C000313102

WALKS

NORTHAMPTONSHIRE

CHERYL JOYCE

BRADWELL
BOOKS

WALKS FOR ALL AGES

NORTHAMPTONSHIRE

CHERYL JOYCE

BRADWELL
BOOKS

Published by Bradwell Books

9 Orgreave Close Sheffield S13 9NP

Email: books@bradwellbooks.co.uk

British Library Cataloguing in Publication Data: a catalogue record for this book is available from the British Library.

1st Edition

ISBN: 9781902674537

Print: Gomer Press, Llandysul, Ceredigion SA44 4JL

Design by: Erik Siewko Creative, Derbyshire.

eriksiewko@gmail.com

Photograph Credits: © Cheryl Joyce

Maps: Contain Ordnance Survey data © Crown copyright and database right 2013

CONTENTS

INTRODUCTION

Northamptonshire is often said to be an undiscovered county, in terms of its unique history, wildlife and landscapes. Walkers in particular are spoilt for choice, and apart from coastal or perhaps mountain walking, there is much on offer. You will discover ancient wooded areas, river valleys and historic landscapes, and see some amazing views over rolling countryside.

As the title suggests, the walks in this book should be suitable for everyone, especially families and those new to walking. They range in length from just under 2 miles to 6 miles, and are spread throughout the county so that you get a taste of all the varied scenery it has to offer.

The routes mainly follow rights of way such as footpaths and bridleways. Walking along roads has been avoided as far as possible, and any sections you do find will be short, and with little traffic. Even so, take care, particularly when out with children or dogs. For all the walks, keeping dogs on a lead is not obligatory but is recommended, especially as many of the fields are pasture land and are quite likely to have grazing livestock in them, sometimes with young.

The route map and directions should get you safely from start to finish, but please be aware that things change over time. For example, occasionally footpaths are diverted or stiles are replaced by gates. It is always helpful to take the relevant Ordnance Survey map with you, as back up. These maps will also give you additional information about the area you are walking through.

A walker should never be too far from refreshment, so do carry a drink and a snack with you, even on the shortest of walks. It is easy to get engrossed in the scenery or have an unexpected stop to meander around a churchyard, and before you know it you've been out twice as long as expected. Local hostelries and other places of refreshment are noted in the "The Basics", but the list is not exhaustive, and does not indicate any preference one over another. You should check their opening times before setting out.

The good old British climate can be relied upon to be unreliable, so carrying some lightweight waterproofs at all times makes sense. Also make sure you have good walking boots. Even after prolonged dry periods you may find yourself walking over permanently marshy ground, or along a stubbornly muddy path.

Finally, and perhaps most importantly, enjoy yourself! The unique and lovely Northamptonshire countryside is out there, waiting for you.

ABINGTON PARK

This route is entirely on surfaced paths. There are some slight inclines, but the route is entirely suitable for buggies. There are two road crossings, one of which is a pelican crossing; and a short section of pavement walking.

Abington Park is 117 acres in size and is Northampton's oldest and most popular park. It has many facilities on offer, such as the museum, bowling greens, tennis courts, and cricket and football pitches. You will walk past pretty flower beds, two lakes, some aviaries and a café. In 2012 a leading travel and tourism website rated it as one of the top five parks in the UK.

The park, created by the Thursby family, was opened to the public in 1897, followed two years later by the opening of Abington Museum. In 1900 the bandstand was put in place, and it has been used ever since, with dozens of concerts taking place every year.

Bandstand

Amazingly, there are 352 different species of tree in Abington Park, which is the second largest amount you will find anywhere in England, beaten only by Kew Gardens.

The archaeological remains of the medieval Abington village lie beneath the surface of the park, and some of the buildings in it are more than seven centuries old! One such building is the medieval manor house with its mill attached. The village became depopulated when the manor was enlarged. Two old gate posts from the village still remain, so see if you can spot them on this walk.

The Sensory Garden

The Church of St Peter and St Paul dates back to the 13th century. In 1981 a coffin was found in a vault beneath the Lady Chapel. This turned out to be that of William Shakespeare's granddaughter Elizabeth Bernard. Elizabeth lived in Abington Manor house and was buried here in 1670.

The Abington gallows were thought to have been situated at the crossroads in the park. Their most notorious use was for the hanging of five women following the Northamptonshire witch trials in 1612.

The museum is well worth a visit. Amongst the displays on offer are those on the Northamptonshire Regiment and Yeomanry, and also the story of the county's shoe-making industry.

Once you have walked in the park a few times you may feel confident to alter your route and find new places to explore.

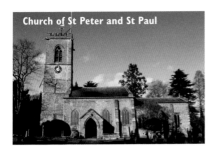

Church of St Peter and St Paul

THE BASICS

Distance in miles and km: 1.75 miles (3 km)

Gradient: Some short inclines but mainly flat level going

Severity: Easy

Approx min time to walk: 0.75 hr – 1.25 hrs

Stiles: None

Maps: OS Explorer 207

Path description: Mainly tarmacced paths. A short section of pavement

Start Point: Park gates opposite Abington Hotel, NN1 4EY

Parking: Roads alongside park

Dog friendly: On leads for preference

Public Toilets: On south side of park, close to café and bowling greens

Nearest food: Park café, open daily

ABINGTON PARK WALK

1) Abington Park has many entrances. This walk starts from the gates on the corner of Wellingborough Road and Ardington Road, opposite the Abington Hotel. Go through the gates and take the wide path straight ahead of you (do not go either right or left). You are heading for a lovely honey-coloured stone building and church. As you approach you may hear lots of cheeping before you see that Abington Park Aviaries are on your left. You can have a look now or towards the end of the walk, when we pass close by once again. You will come to Abington Park Museum. At the third flower bed go right down a small path which takes you to the church. At the fork continue right and right again to a road.

2) Be careful crossing this fairly busy road. Take the path on the opposite side and walk down a gentle hill through an avenue of trees, including beech, oak and sycamore. You will pass some football pitches on your right — some of the many facilities the park has to offer.

3) At the lake and junction of paths take a right, passing a wooded area of mainly native species, at the end becoming a screen of tall bamboo right next to the small lake. Walk to the end of the lake and take the path bearing right, up to the road.

4) Turn left and walk up the pavement, passing pine trees and ivy-covered sycamore trees, and also some very old iron railings. After roughly 300m (300 yards) you reach a path on your left, opposite Weston Way, going back into the park.

5) Walk down hill between another avenue of trees, until you reach another lake. Here, continue ahead, keeping the railings to the right. As you pass the lake you may wish to take a seat and watch the waterfowl, with species like coots, mallards, moorhens and black-headed gulls to look at.

6) Where the path forks, go right up a short incline and continue to a bench. You will notice a honey-coloured tower to your right, which was probably a dovecote. Feel free to wander off the path to go and have a closer look. Pigeons often sit in the various nooks and crannies. Just before the bench take a left and pass in front of the rectangular boating lake. At the end turn left and walk down to the duck lake again. At the lake turn right and walk alongside it, to where a path comes in from the right.

7) Go up here and up the slight hill, ignoring a path that comes in from the right. You will pass some gym equipment, which is part of the fitness trail around the park. Continue up the hill, past a children's play area with lots of exciting equipment to play on. When you get to the road, cross over by way of the pelican crossing, and walk up past the museum, which will be on your

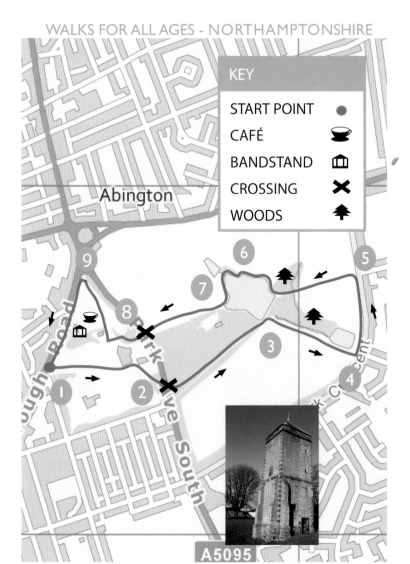

left. You will soon see the café in front of you, so if you need refreshment, now is the time to take some. The aviaries are also close by.

8) At the path junction turn right and walk along, keeping the café and flower beds to your left. Walk ahead until you almost reach the gate at the roadside, then turn left here.

9) Follow the path, with the wall to your right. Pass a sculpture made from an old tree stump and then a strange mound with a sycamore tree growing out of it, exposing its lovely roots. Past some holly bushes, and then the bandstand on your left. Continue to the gates where you started from.

GRENDON

This walk passes close to Castle Ashby village and gives you tantalising views of the impressive Castle Ashby House. It then takes you through the very quaint Easton Maudit village and back up to Grendon.

It is an easy walk but does have three stiles and a few gentle inclines. Almost the entire route is on unsurfaced tracks, which may be muddy after rain. It affords some lovely views across a very quiet part of the county.

Start Here

Grendon means "green hill" and even today the village remains centred on the hill. The village was once owned by Countess Judith, William the Conqueror's niece. There are several thatched cottages and the pub, the Half Moon, is also thatched.

The parish church, St Mary's, dates back to Roman times, and is built from ironstone

St Mary's

rubble. Inside the church are medieval wooden carvings of the grotesque faces of a nagging wife and her leering husband. The inspiration for these carvings is thought to have come from a local couple, who clearly enjoyed a good argument!

Historically, Castle Ashby village was built to service the needs of Castle Ashby Manor. The impressive house was rebuilt in the late 16th and early 17th centuries, and is the seat of the Marquis of Northampton. There are several events in the grounds each year, including concerts and the Country Fair, a popular event which raises funds for local community needs. Castle Ashby gardens are open all year round and are well worth a visit. The tea room there is open between April and September. There is also Castle Ashby Shopping Yard in the village, with craft shops and another café, the Buttery.

Until 1131 Easton Maudit was simply called Easton. It was then purchased by the Mauduit family and took on its current name. The Great Tree on the triangle at the end of the village was an oak, and lived to be many hundreds of years old. It died in the

Grendon Copse

1990s, and was replaced by a hornbeam, which is thriving. John Bunyan and Charles Wesley are reputed to have preached under the Great Tree.

The Church of St Peter and St Paul has a lovely spire. The actor Derek Nimmo lived in Easton Maudit, and is buried in the churchyard. The village once had a manor house, but when the Compton family from Castle Ashby bought it they demolished it. All that remains are the cedars of Lebanon which once surrounded it, which you will see when you pass by the church.

Old Tree at Easton Maudit

Easton Maudit Church

Cottage near Parkhill

THE BASICS

Distance in miles and km: 5 miles (8 km)

Gradient: Some short inclines but mainly flat level going

Severity: Easy

Approx min time to walk: 2 – 2.5 hours

Stiles: I double and I single

Maps: OS Landranger 152 or Explorer 207

Path description: Mainly footpaths & bridleways, some quiet road walking

Start Point: Footpath in Grendon SP876603 NN7 IJE

Parking: Roadside near to start

Dog friendly: On leads for preference

Public Toilets: None on route, nearest at Castle Ashby tearooms

Nearest food: Castle Ashby tearooms, or Half Moon pub in Grendon

GRENDON WALK

1) At the 5–7 Manor Court cul-de-sac, look right to see a footpath sign, pointing down between two buildings. Go down here and through a kissing gate. Turn left and walk across this ridge and furrow field, to the hedge. Go over a double stile, and take the path going diagonally right (not the one next to the fence), and cross the field. You can see the imposing Castle Ashby House in the distance straight ahead.

2) Go over the footbridge and head straight across the field, passing a small copse of trees on your right. When you reach the road, you can clearly see Castle Ashby House directly ahead of you. This will be your closest view of it. Turn left and

Footbridge

walk up the road, soon passing a lovely stand of Scots pine on your right, by a house. Continue along the road, passing Parkhill Offices on your left.

3) When you reach the road junction turn right, towards Yardley Hastings. Soon you come to a bridleway on your left. Follow this across the field, to a bridge over a stream. Continue along the bridleway, slightly uphill and with a hedge with many lime trees to your left. Go through the gap

and continue to the road. There are good views of the surrounding countryside during this section, and you can see Cold Oak Copse and Hill's Copse to your right, in the distance.

4) Cross the road and continue on the path, which bends gently to the left. This is great skylark country, and you may hear one trilling or see it soaring. Go through the gate into the pasture, keeping close to the hedge on your right, until you reach Easton Maudit village.

5) At the road turn left and walk up the street, past some fine old cottages. Continue ahead to the church, in front of which is the huge trunk of an old oak tree. At the church turn left then immediately right, down the footpath. There are several beautiful cedar of Lebanon trees here, and you pass right under one as you walk along the track.

6) Go through the gate and follow the path round to the right, towards some old farm buildings. Go through another gate and pass to the left of these old buildings. You soon come to a wooden footbridge on your right. Turn left here and head diagonally right across the field to a gateway with another ruined building. Cross the next field diagonally right again, to the corner, where you'll find a footbridge which takes you over the stream.

7) Once again cross the next field

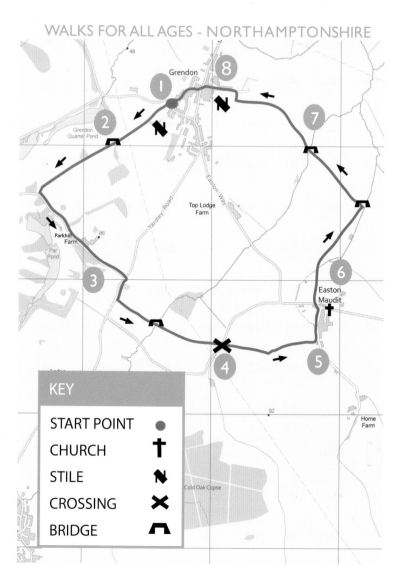

KEY

START POINT	●
CHURCH	✝
STILE	⊼
CROSSING	✕
BRIDGE	⌒

diagonally, to a metal hand gate. Look back where you've come from, to admire the lovely views. Continue straight on, keeping the hedge to your right. Go through a wooden hand gate, across the field and soon through a metal gate, admiring Grendon church to your right. After approximately 20 yards (20m) you'll see a stile on your right. Cross this and continue straight on to the kissing gate by the road — Chequers Lane.

8) Turn left here and carry on up towards the church. At the junction, cross over and walk through the churchyard, down to the road. On your right is Little Hall, with a coat of arms over the door. Go straight over the road and follow the footpath sign, which takes you past Blacksmith's Cottage on your left, through an alleyway and out by the school. Continue up the road till you reach the junction, then turn right and walk back to the start.

ISLIP

This walk takes you on a meander through the picturesque Nene Valley, with great opportunities to see wildlife, particularly wetland birds. At one point you are walking with a lake either side of you, one of which is a nature reserve.

There are several bird hides in the reserve, so feel free to stop at any of them and go in and see what wildlife is around. The walk is mainly on level ground, and has three low stiles.

Into the Nature Reserve

Islip village is situated to the west of Thrapston, and they are separated only by the River Nene. You have to cross over the Nine Arch Bridge to get from one to the other. One idea about what Islip means is "slippery bank of the River Ise". This is somewhat puzzling as the River Nene is far closer; the River Ise actually runs several miles to the west of Islip. One can only assume that they looked at the landscape in a very different way in those days.

Islip Mill

John Washington, the great, great, great uncle of the first American president George Washington, lived in nearby Thrapston, and his wife Mary is buried in Islip church.

Islip Mill, now derelict, had two water-wheels and was working up until 1960, when it sadly fell into disrepair.

Aldwincle is unusual in having two churches: All Saints and St Peter's. This is because it was once much larger than it is today, and was then made up of two parishes. Today there are about 350 souls in the village. All Saints is no longer used regularly, but a church service is held there every year, on or near All Saints' Day. The village rectory opposite All Saints was where the poet John Dryden was born, in 1631.

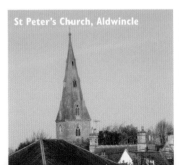
St Peter's Church, Aldwincle

St Peter's is an attractive church with a beautiful broach spire, and lovely stained-glass windows. The nearby Baulks Lane, which is part of this walk, was once used for funeral processions to St Peter's Church.

Titchmarsh local nature reserve is managed by the Beds, Cambs and Northants Wildlife Trusts. It is an important site for migrating waterfowl and those which over-winter, as are many of the former gravel pits along the River Nene corridor. Titchmarsh reserve has a heronry where many herons breed. The collective noun for herons is a "parliament", and one can imagine these very upright and stately birds musing and muttering together – very much like politicians!

Elinor Lake

THE BASICS

Distance in miles and km: 5 miles (8 km)

Gradient: Some short inclines but mainly flat, level going

Severity: Easy; alongside river and lakes, through open countryside

Approx min time to walk: 2 – 2.5 hours

Stiles: None

Maps: OS Landranger 141 & Explorer 224

Path description: Mainly footpaths and unmade track (byway)

Start Point: Rose and Crown pub, Islip SP 988792 NN14 3LB

Parking: On Mill Road or High St, Islip

Dog friendly: On leads for preference

Public Toilets: Rose & Crown, or Pear Tree Farm tearooms

Nearest food: Woolpack Inn, Islip or Pear Tree Farm tearooms

1) Follow the Nene Way down past the left-hand side of the Rose and Crown, through the car park and picnic area, to the bottom. After the gate bear left across a grassed area with stepping stones, to a kissing gate. Once through the gate bear slightly right, across to the corner of the field.

2) Cross the road. If you wish, take a quick detour to the river and look at the disused Islip Mill. Then, keeping the ruined barn close to your left, follow the Nene Way footpath across the fields. Cross a concrete bridge over a stream, with a fine old pollarded ash tree in the hedge to your left. Continue to a footbridge in the corner.

3) Go over the bridge into the wood, and turn right immediately, following the path through the wood (occasionally orange tape is up, which you can go around). There are some lovely large wych elms in the wood. Their leaves are very distinctive, and easily recognised by the uneven junction with the leaf stem. Go over a footbridge, emerging by a large poplar tree and metal bridge.

4) Turn left through the gate and into Titchmarsh Local Nature Reserve. Walk ahead to a fence corner with a footpath either side. Continue ahead, keeping the fence to your right. At the bend go right, following the Nene Way as it passes between two lakes. Notice the devices on the power lines overhead, which make

them more visible in order to prevent birds flying into them. Go through the gate. Sheep sometimes graze this area, to keep down invasive scrub so that the wild flowers can flourish.

5) When Elinor Lake to your left ends, continue on through a kissing gate and onto a section of boardwalk. Pass through a gate with a hide on the right. Follow the path as it winds its way to a car park, going through two kissing gates and across a bridge on the way.

6) At the car park turn right and walk down the road, passing a pumping station on the right. At Grange House you'll see a footpath called Baulks Lane. Follow this to the top, passing under a walnut tree on the right, to come to the village green, complete with memorial, information panel and old hawthorn tree. Right next to the green is Pear Tree Farm tearooms, for rest and refreshment.

7) Continue past the tearoom and take the first footpath on the left, opposite Trinity Lower School. Go down a concrete track to a gate and cross diagonally to the next gate. Bear slightly right across the ridge and furrow field, to a gate in the corner. At the road bear left and walk on the verge to the corner, where you'll see a sign for Elinor Trout Fishery and Cottages.

8) Follow the footpath on the road

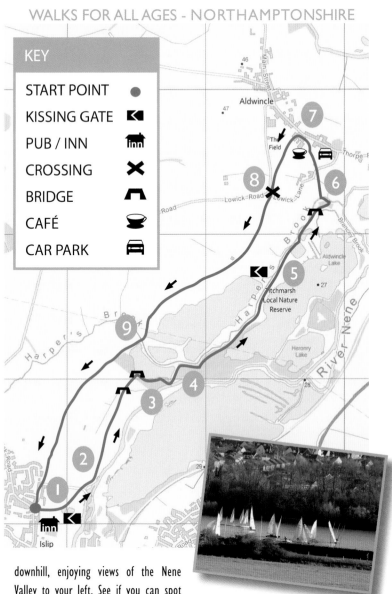

KEY

START POINT	●
KISSING GATE	◪
PUB / INN	⌂
CROSSING	✕
BRIDGE	⌒
CAFÉ	☕
CAR PARK	🚗

downhill, enjoying views of the Nene Valley to your left. See if you can spot Titchmarsh church on the horizon. At Elinor holiday cottages go through the hand gate to the right, and walk along the right-hand side of the grass field. There is a fence on the right – when this comes to an end keep straight on, then bear left under the pylons to an arched bridge by some willow trees. This crosses Harpers Brook.

9) Go straight ahead along the Ridge Road, admiring Bullick's Wood on the rise to the right as you do so. Later you will see Thrapston Lake to your left, where sometimes sail boats can be seen. Eventually you come back into Islip, at Mill Lane. Continue ahead until you are back at the start.

TWYWELL

This is a medium-length walk but is slightly more challenging in nature. This is due to the five stiles along the route, and also three sets of steps down, one of which comprises 48 steps down a fairly steep railway embankment.

However, the steps are well made and all three sets of steps have hand rails. You will be walking them all going downhill, too, if that helps!

Drayton Manor

The optional detour to Drayton House is less than a mile and is well worth it, as the beautiful architecture and impressive lime tree avenue stay in the mind for a long while afterwards.

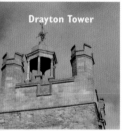
Drayton Tower

The core of the house was built in 1300 by Sir Simon de Drayton, and still survives. There have been changes to the house each century ever since, engineered by many famous architects including Isaac Rowe, William Rhodes and George Devey. In 1770 the house passed to the Sackville family. Today it has many fascinating medieval and Baroque features, to name a few, and is amazingly still a family home.

Twywell is recorded in the Domesday Book as Twowelle — that is, two wells — but it can be dated back to the Iron Age. Manor House Farm, where the walk begins, dates from 1591. Some of the building material used for the farm is thought to have been reclaimed from an old monastery situated between Slipton and Sudborough, at a site known as "Money Holes". Nobody knows the reason behind this name, but there are a lot of stone pits in the area, so perhaps this is where fortunes were made!

Manor Farm Barn

Steps Down

Twywell was the birthplace of the bluestocking writer Hester Chapone, who wrote a book to her fifteen-year-old niece telling her how she should behave. Perhaps she was going through a rebellious stage! The book was called "Letters on the Improvement of the Mind" and clearly caught some sort of cultural wave, as it remained influential and was regularly reprinted for over fifty years.

Twywell Hills and Dales Country Park is nearby, and is popular with villagers as it is only a short walk away. There are several waymarked walks within the park. It is a former quarry site, and part of the park is a Site of Special Scientific Interest because of the richness of its wildlife, particularly pond life.

Red Brick House

THE BASICS

Distance in miles and km: 3 miles (5 km).
(Optional detour 3.5 miles (6 km))

Gradient: Few short inclines but 3 sets of steps (downhill)

Severity: Slightly more difficult – due to 3 sets of steps and 5 Stiles

Approx min time to walk: 1.5 – 2 hours

Stiles: 5

Maps: OS Landranger 141 or Explorer 224

Path description: Mainly footpaths across fields, and surfaced tracks

Start Point: Manor Farm, Twywell, in centre of village SP 951784 NN14 3AH

Parking: Side of road near Manor Farm, opposite The Green

Dog friendly: On leads for preference

Public Toilets: None on route, nearest in Thrapston

Nearest food: The Old Friar, Twywell, or Samuel Pepys, Slipton

1) Although Manor Farm isn't named, you can't miss it as it is almost opposite The Green and has an imposing, stone-pillared entrance. Go through the entrance and immediately bear left, through the farmyard and past a Dutch barn on the right, then through a metal gate. Go straight ahead to a gap and then carry straight on towards a small spinney, which is actually an old railway cutting.

2) Go over the stile then down the 48 steps to the stream. Cross the bridge and over the stile, then head slightly left up the gentle hill. When you reach the horizon look for a line of trees with a stile to the left of them. Go over the stile and down the five steps to the road.

3) Cross the road and go down the five steps into the field. Continue over the next two fields, reaching a small wooded area where quarrying took place. All the pits and workings have been re-colonised by trees and shrubs.

4) Pass through the trees and up the short incline. Continue straight on, keeping the hedge to the right. At the next field continue ahead, with the hedge to your right. Look out for red kites soaring overhead.

5) Once you reach the road/track, you now have the option to detour to visit Drayton House. (If not taking the detour, skip to (7)). If you wish to detour, turn right here, then immediately left, past two stone houses. Follow the track down, watching Drayton House coming into view. You will pass two magnificent Wellingtonia trees on the right.

6) Drayton House in all its glory is now in front of you, with an avenue of tall lime trees just to its left. The footpath continues on the tarmac road passing in front of the house and round to the right, past Gardener's Cottage. Once reaching the cattle grid you should turn around, and retrace your steps past Drayton House. This gives you another opportunity to admire the amazing architecture of the buildings. Walk back up past the stone cottages, to where your footpath emerged from the field. Continue straight on.

7) If you aren't taking the detour, turn left at the track. Go past the red-bricked Home Farm, with a lovely white gate in the privet hedge. The road bends round to the left and you can now see Slipton village in the distance, and several wind turbines on the horizon. Enjoy the views as you follow the road around a couple more bends.

8) When you are close to Slipton village look out for a white Drayton Estate sign with its back to you, by a track to the left and a sign saying "Church". Take this track and go through the wooden

Drayton House

KEY

START POINT	●
CHURCH	✝
STILE	N
CROSSING	✕
BRIDGE	⌐
STEPS	◣
MANOR HOUSE	🏠

gate into the churchyard. Follow the concrete path around to the left of the church, passing a memorial for the First World War. Continue through another gate and out onto a grass track. Follow the track into Slipton.

9) At the road turn left and walk to the junction. Turn left again, past the Samuel Pepys country pub. Opposite the pub is a footpath sign. The path goes up someone's drive, through a small green gate and out into a field. Go straight ahead to a stile in the distance. Then straight on again, heading for a metal gate. You will emerge at a bend in the road.

10) Immediately turn left and over a stile, then walk straight ahead, keeping the hedge close to your left. At the straggly row of trees you will rejoin the footpath you took out of Twywell, so here you must turn right and head towards the red barn of Manor Farm. Go through the gate and into the farmyard, and back out onto the road, and where you started from.

POLEBROOK

This walk takes in some of the gently rolling countryside in the north of the county, and affords views of the nearby Ashton Wold woodlands and the River Nene valley. About half of the walk is on surfaced roads and tracks which are rights of way, and have very little traffic.

The village of Polebrook, with its stone cottages with thatched or Collyweston slate roofs, is very pretty. The original settlement was probably established at least a thousand years ago. At the time of the Domesday Survey (1086) it was listed as Pochebroc, which means Goblin Brook. Most of the village lies to the north of the Goblin Brook, although newer development has taken place to the south.

All Saints Church

The Church of All Saints has several stained-glass windows, including one in memory of a Lifeguardsman who fell in the First World War. There is also a roll of honour listing the American servicemen who were killed in the Second World War, who flew from the Polebrook airbase (a couple of miles east of the village).

Servicemen from the 351st Bombardment Group of the US Army Air Force occupied the airbase from 1943 to 1945. The most famous of these was Clark Gable, the film star. From here over 300 aerial missions were flown over occupied Europe.

A quick detour takes you to Polebrook Hall which is originally Jacobean. The wrought iron gates at the entrance date back to the 18th century, and the two pillars each used to have a figure atop them, although now only one remains. The great grandparents of the current Duchess of York lived here for over 50 years.

The hamlet of Armston was also listed in the Domesday Book, and was very tiny even then. The original settlement was abandoned at least once, only to be re-inhabited later. Unfortunately what was left of the original hamlet has been poorly preserved, although large quantities of medieval pottery have been found in the area.

Polebrook Hall

You are very likely to see and hear pheasants on this walk, as well as rooks, crows and jackdaws. The jackdaw is the smallest of these, and makes a characteristic "jack, jack" sound. Polebrook itself is favoured by swifts and swallows, and on sunny days from May to August the air is full of them wheeling around on the hunt for insects. So remember to look up!

Barn Owl Box

Distance in miles and km: 2.5 miles (4 km)

Gradient: Some short inclines but mainly flat level going

Severity: Easy

Approx min time to walk: 1.5 hours

Stiles: None

Maps: OS Landranger 142 or Explorer 227

Path description: Mainly footpaths and surfaced roads

Start Point: Polebrook church TL 068871 PE8 5LN

Parking: In village, on road close to church

Dog friendly: On leads for preference

Public Toilets: Nearest at King's Arms or Olive Grove nursery

Nearest food: King's Arms or Olive Grove nursery

POLEBROOK WALK

1) Starting from All Saints Church, take the Hemington Road down the slight hill, away from the centre of the village. Go over the Goblin Brook and past some recently built houses on the right, with interesting names such as Merryburn and Gallica House. Continue until you see Roberts Lane on the right. Go down this rather potholed road for a short distance, then turn left. This next stretch of lane is lovely and peaceful and has very infrequent traffic.

2) Note a footpath sign on your right (you will use this to return), but for now carry on up the road as it winds very gently uphill. If you look across the field to the right you may see a little house on a pole — a barn owl box. These are often in pairs, as it is said that after mating male and female barn owls prefer separate accommodation! And indeed, there is another barn owl box to spot later on. Boxes are put up because of the lack of old trees with suitable holes in, or decrepit barns to use for nesting.

3) Continue ahead past a spinney on the right, and then a field on the left where there are often lovely Dexter cows grazing. These cows are friendly, small, dual-purpose beasts (good for both meat and milk), and are often favoured by smallholders. The road bends to the right and as you near the village, if you are eagle-eyed you may be able to spot the second barn owl box in the hedge of the field to the right.

4) As you come into Armston village you can see Horse Close Spinney on your right, with a good number of elm trees in it. Armston Hall Farm is on your left, with a door surrounded by creepers at the top of some steps. The owners must have a sense of humour, judging by the notice on the front gate! Continue through the village past the farm buildings on your left, then finally Armston Lodge on the right.

5) You will now see a footpath sign on your right, opposite a magnificent old oak tree. Follow the footpath across the ridge and furrow field, bearing slightly right and heading for a V-shaped wooden structure in the hedge. Go over this footbridge and diagonally across the arable field, aiming for some white buildings over in Polebrook. You will now be able to clearly see the spire of All Saints Church, and you can also see Ashton Wold Wood on the hill in the distance. The path brings you to a grass headland which sticks out into the field. Go down this grass path to a footbridge and cross over.

War Memorial

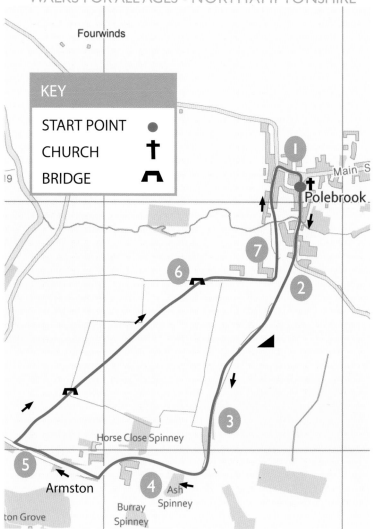

6) Now turn right, soon passing a fenced area on your left, and walk to the end. You emerge where you passed by earlier. Here, turn left and walk to the junction. Opposite is a gap by a wooden gate.

7) Go through here and walk through some rough grassland, with plenty of brambles. This sheltered area is a haven for butterflies and bees, and the

brambles provide plenty of nectar for them to feed on. Follow the track up past the cottages and to the King's Arms pub. Now turn right and walk to the war memorial. If you want to explore the village, Polebrook Hall is a little further up on the right. Otherwise, just turn right here and you are back at the church.

NASSINGTON

This is a pleasant walk taking in the River Nene and a small nature reserve, with lots of variety. You will follow the Nene Way county footpath for part of the route, then after this you will be on parish footpaths and a small section of byway.

The walk is well waymarked and very nearly flat all the way, with only a couple of slight inclines to tackle. As there is a small section close to the river, be aware that this part may flood after prolonged periods of rain.

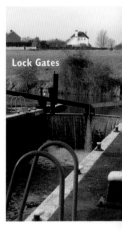
Lock Gates

The Nassington area is rich in archaeology, and was evidently occupied thousands of years ago. The remains of several prehistoric barrows have been found nearby, plus the remains of a Roman village, together with evidence of its iron-working industry. Nassington church has Saxon origins, and you can see the base of a Saxon cross in the churchyard.

13th CENTURY
PREBENDAL MANOR
OPEN EASTER MON
TO END OF SEPTEMBER
BANK HOLIDAY
MONS, WEDS & SUNS
2.00pm -5.30pm

The Prebendal Manor House was built in 1230, and is the oldest occupied house in Northamptonshire. It is a Grade I listed building, and there is also a 16th-century dovecote and a large 18th-century tithe barn. These are all open to the public on certain days between Easter and October – check out the website (www.prebendal-manor.co.uk) for visiting times.

There are several theories as to where the name Yarwell comes from. Some say it was the place where the wild herb called Yarrow grows, and as at one time nearly every house in the village had a well, this gave rise to the name Yarwell.

Yarwell Mill

Back in the day there were several mills operating in Yarwell, using water from the River Nene to power them. One was a paper mill, producing paper for newspapers, including The Times. However, an explosion in the mill in 1855 put an end to the business. As you walk towards Yarwell you may hear the whistle and puffing of a steam train, and may smell the coal smoke from its chimney. The Nene Valley Railway passes very close to Yarwell, although it is difficult to actually spot a train as they are only visible for a very short space of time.

Yarwell Village Hall Committee has offered tea and cakes every Sunday afternoon in summer for many years. All monies raised go towards looking after the village hall, so if you happen to be walking here on a summer Sunday afternoon do go and have a cuppa!

A Narrow Path

The Angel Inn

THE BASICS

Distance in miles and km: 4 miles (6.5 km)

Gradient: Some short inclines but mainly flat level going

Severity: Easy

Approx min time to walk: 1.5 – 2 hours

Stiles: 3

Maps: OS Landranger 142 & Explorer 227

Path description: Footpaths, byways, and a short section of pavement

Start Point: Black Horse Inn, Nassington TL 067962 PE8 6QU

Parking: In village, near to start

Dog friendly: On leads for preference

Public Toilets: None on route, nearest at Black Horse Inn

Nearest food: Black Horse Inn, Nassington

NASSINGTON WALK

1) Starting at the Black Horse Inn, cross the road to a Nene Way footpath sign and follow the path through the field, ignoring a track veering to the right. You will pass some large willow trees on your right-hand side. Go through the gate, over the River Nene and across the next field, keeping close to the hedge on your right. Go straight over the next field.

2) After two kissing gates you will be walking along quite close the Nene. Go through a gap in metal railings and follow the path, ignoring a footbridge over the river on your right. You will pass by a small plantation of poplar trees. At the gate walk up a shady path towards a lock in the river. Cross over, and head towards Yarwell Mill.

3) Pass in front of the mill and follow the road around to the left. Just after the barrier, take the footpath and walk along the edge of the field, noticing the mill and caravan site to your right. Then veer diagonally across the next field, to come out at Yarwell.

4) At this point you have the option to explore the village, in which case just turn right here and have a wander! Otherwise, take the footpath opposite and walk to the end. Here turn right then quickly left, and carry on up past the recreation ground and some allotments, noticing the lovely tower of Yarwell Church on your right as you do so. Continue ahead, crossing over the road and the next field, up a very gentle incline, to a stile in the hedge.

5) Continue to a footbridge, followed by a low stile. Keep going, ignoring a footpath heading off to the right. Go through a gap in the hedge and walk along a narrow path with a fence ether side. At the end of this go through a gate, turn right, and go downhill to the track.

6) Here turn left and go downhill, passing through an area with rampant wild clematis or "old man's beard" on the trees and bushes. At Ring Haw Field station take a moment to read the Old Sulehay panel, for some interesting information about the area. Carry on up the byway, ignoring the metal gate on your left, until you see a crooked byway sign on the right. On the left just after this is the gate you should go through.

7) Follow the footpath downhill through some rough grassland. In summer this area is rich in birds and butterflies, which feed on the wild flowers. Go through a wooden gate and straight over the next field. Turn right at a broken wooden fence and cross over the disused railway. At the gate turn left, and after two more gates follow a well-

Yarwell Church

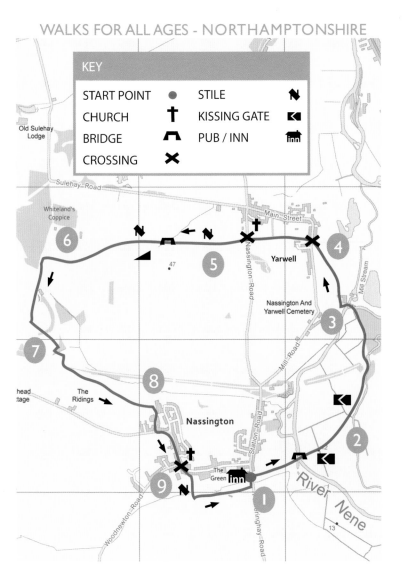

defined path across a grass field. At the end go through the gate and up to the top.

8) Turn right and walk to the road junction. Turn left at the phone box and then right at Church Street. Walk to the church, passing the old thatched cottage called Three Mill Bills as you do so. Go through the churchyard, taking time to look at the old gravestones and enjoy the architecture of this imposing church.

9) At the end, cross the road to the track between the two houses opposite. (To detour to the Prebendal Manor House, turn right here and find it a little further up on the left). Go down the track over a stile and past an old railway signal to the end. Here turn left. Follow this path past a playground and the cricket club, all the way back to the start.

MAIDWELL

This walk is a very pleasant, mainly flat stroll through the Brampton Valley. Part of it follows the linear route of the Brampton Valley Way, and is surfaced. The rest of it follows footpaths, with a small amount of pavement walking in the village.

The Brampton Valley Way is based upon a disused railway line. It was once a busy rural branch line owned by the London and North Western Railway company, and ran between Northampton and Market Harborough. It first opened in 1859, and served passengers for over one hundred years, closing first to the public in the 1960s and finally closing to freight traffic in 1981.

Turn left for Maidwell

Northamptonshire County Council bought the railway line in 1987 with money from the Countryside Commission, with the idea of developing it into a linear park, which indeed is what they did. They created a route suitable for wheelchairs, walkers and

Bridleway

cyclists alike, and in some places horse riders are catered for, too. It is very popular with young families as it is pretty flat, and is traffic-free for its entire length. The Council has provided facilities such as car parks, picnic sites and benches at various intervals along the route.

There are tunnels along the route at Kelmarsh and Great Oxendon, which are north of Maidwell. You will not visit them during this walk, but they are well worth exploring at a later date. The former is 462 yards (422m) long and the latter is 322 yards (294m). The tunnels are unlit and it is a strange experience walking through them in the dark — so taking a torch is recommended. For the less intrepid there is a route over the length of the tunnel, should this be required.

Maidwell Hall, an independent prep school, was bought by Oliver Wyatt in 1933, to establish it as his home and as a school. You can still see the gates to his house if you walk from the church to the Stag's Head — the sign says "Wyatt's Place". The Hall is certainly very interesting architecturally, and the grounds were once equally beautiful and quite famous, since the previous

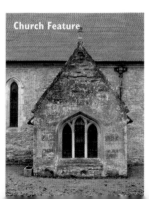
Church Feature

owner had been a prominent plantsman. Occasionally the public are allowed into the grounds for events, such as the annual village cricket match. Otherwise, all you can do is view this collection of buildings with its towers and chimneys from the churchyard, and imagine what it was like in its heyday.

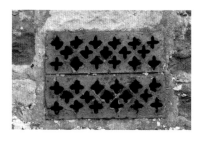

Rectory Farmhouse with Gargoyle

Maidwell Church

THE BASICS

Distance in miles and km: 2.5 miles (4 km)

Gradient: Almost entirely level

Severity: Easy

Approx min time to walk: 1.25 – 1.75 hours

Stiles: None

Maps: OS Landranger 141 & Explorer 223

Path description: Mainly footpaths and disused railway bed

Start Point: Draughton Crossing car park SP 755774 NN6 9JF

Parking: Free car park

Dog friendly: On leads for preference

Public Toilets: None on route, nearest at Stag's Head, Maidwell

Nearest food: Stag's Head Inn, Maidwell

MAIDWELL WALK

1) From Draughton Crossing car park follow the signs along the Brampton Valley Way north towards Kelmarsh. The entire Brampton Valley Way is part of the Sustrans (Sustainable Transport) National Cycle Network, which in this case runs between Northampton and Market Harborough, so you may see cyclists from time to time. The going is flat and easy, allowing you plenty of opportunity to look up at the surrounding countryside.

2) You will come to where a bridleway crosses the path, known as Green Lane Crossing. It is here that you should turn left towards Maidwell village. Follow the bridleway between two arable fields as it gently bends to the left and goes up a slight rise. This will give you more great views across the Brampton Valley. When you come to a metal gate turn left and go down the grass verge, keeping the hedge on your right, heading towards the village.

3) Go through the next field gate where you will see a magnificent oak tree in the hedge on the left. It is worth a quick detour to have a proper look at it. Oak trees can live to over a thousand years old (in rare cases), but there are plenty of examples of veteran oaks between four

hundred and six hundred years old in Northamptonshire. Although this is a fine specimen, it is a mere babe, as it is probably somewhere between 120 and 150 years old. Now follow the track as it winds towards the village, and go out the gate and up to the junction.

4) Turn right here and walk down the main street of the village. Look out for Rectory Farmhouse on the right, which has a rather interesting gargoyle on the front door. Pass under a very large beech tree, and then go past Maidwell primary school on the right. The Church of St Mary the Virgin will be in front of you. Feel free to explore the churchyard — from here you get good views of Maidwell Hall, which is now a prep school, and which has many interesting towers and turrets. There is a row of pollarded lime trees alongside the wall of the churchyard. Pollarding is an old practice of cutting the tops of the trees regularly, to keep them to a reasonable size. Otherwise they could grow to well over one hundred feet high.

If you are looking for some refreshment at this point, now is the time to turn right and follow the road down to the main A509, where you will see the Stag's Head public house opposite.

5) By the church there is a waymarker post with "Maidwell Trail" and a Macmillan Way disc on it. This is where you should turn left and go down the

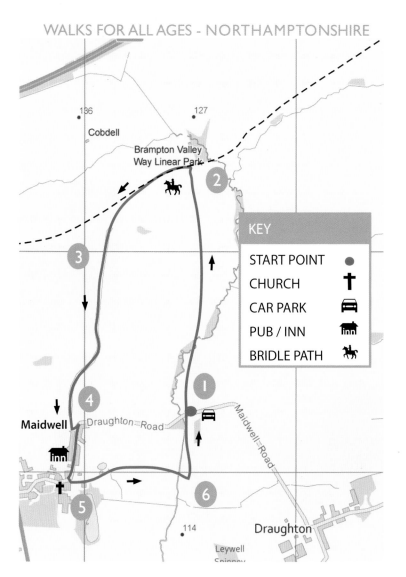

small track. You will go past a blue cedar tree on the right, through a kissing gate and then you should bear left across a field, keeping the ditch to your left initially. You will pass a small spinney of willow trees on your right. Head for the telegraph pole with a waymarker disc on it. Now aim for what looks like a gate in the corner, slightly downhill. It is actually a footbridge, which you cross over and then walk up to a metal railway bridge, which is clearly visible ahead. Go through the kissing gate, and you are now back on the Brampton Valley Way.

6) As you can see on the signs, you are only a quarter of a mile from the car park. So turn left and walk up the track, enjoying your last views of the Brampton Valley countryside.

STOKE BRUERNE

This walk takes you through mostly level countryside around the village of Stoke Bruerne, visiting the neighbouring Shutlanger on the return journey. There is a small amount of road walking on very quiet roads.

The rest of the route follows footpaths and bridleways (which can be muddy after rain) and the canal towpath. There are no steps or stiles on the walk.

The Grand Union Canal is Britain's longest, linking London to Birmingham. The fascinating museum at Stoke Bruerne gives a glimpse into this waterway's past. It was opened in a disused steam mill in 1963, and is still going strong today.

By the towpath

Tunnel Entrance

You can take a narrowboat ride up to the entrance of the Blisworth Tunnel, (although you will walk very close to it on this route). The guide on board tells you all about the history of the tunnel and the canal generally. The tunnel opened in 1805, and is 3,076 yards or 2,813 metres long, making it one of the longest navigable tunnels in the country. When the canal was used less and less it fell into disrepair, and eventually it was closed for safety reasons. The restoration work took a staggering five years to complete. When the tunnel finally re-opened in 1984 five thousand people attended the celebrations, which was the same number as attended its first opening in 1805. There is a section of tunnel on the bank next to the entrance, which gives you an idea of its size.

There is a blacksmith's workshop by the tunnel entrance, where Mr Nightingale makes authentic iron fixtures and fittings for organisations such as English Heritage and the National Trust. He also takes commissions for private work. If he is open, do go in and have a browse.

Blacksmith's wares

For those interested in locks, this section of the canal has seven locks in total, with a fall of 55 feet or 17 metres.

Just outside Stoke Bruerne village is Rookery Open Farm, which gives visitors the opportunity to interact with a wide variety of farm animals. There are picnic areas and a tearoom. It is normally open from March to October.

Shutlanger, originally Shuttlehangar, once had a thriving pillow-lace and shoe manufacturing industry, but is now just a tiny commuter village for Milton Keynes and London. There is still, however, a public house called the Plough, if you are in need of refreshment at this point of the walk. Otherwise there are two pubs and a couple of cafés in Stoke Bruerne, so take your pick!

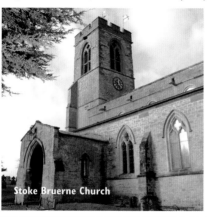

Stoke Bruerne Church

Distance in miles and km: 4 miles (6.5 km)

Gradient: Some short inclines but mainly flat level going

Severity: Easy

Approx min time to walk: 1.5 – 2 hours

Stiles: None

Maps: OS Landranger 152 & Explorer 207

Path description: Towpaths, footpaths, pavements and unmade track

Start Point: Canal Museum, Stoke Bruerne SP 744499 NN12 7SE

Parking: Pay & display car park at Canal Museum, locked at dusk

Dog friendly: On leads for preference

Public Toilets: At Canal Museum

Nearest food: Boat Inn or Navigation Inn, Stoke Bruerne

THE BASICS

STOKE BRUERNE WALK

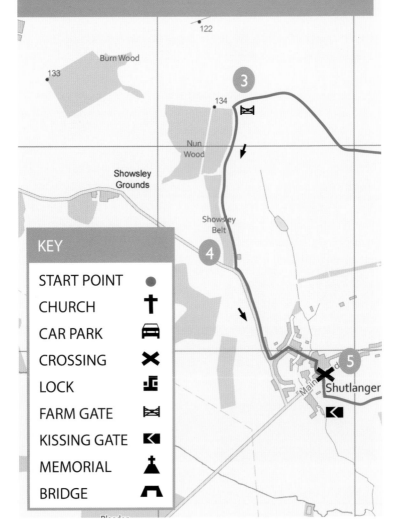

KEY

START POINT	●
CHURCH	†
CAR PARK	🚗
CROSSING	✕
LOCK	🔒
FARM GATE	⛩
KISSING GATE	◄
MEMORIAL	▲
BRIDGE	⌂

1) From the car park, walk up the ramp to the canal. Turn right and walk along the towpath, where there are always colourful canal boats moored up. Follow the signs to Blisworth Tunnel. You can walk right up to the tunnel entrance, passing a blacksmith's workshop, to peer into the darkness. Feel free to have a browse in the blacksmith's if he is open. He makes lots of authentic products for both heritage organisations and private

individuals. Also have a look at the section of tunnel, which is on display on the bank. Then retrace your steps and go up the incline on the woodland walk, following the signs to Blisworth.

2) At the road, walk towards two bridleway signs ahead. Take the one pointing left. This section can be muddy in wet weather. Follow this as it goes through several fields, sometimes with

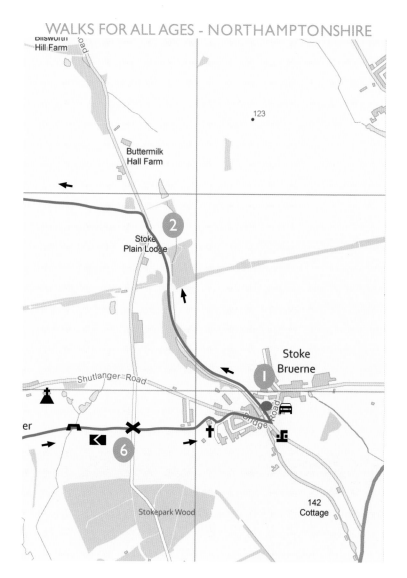

hedges on both sides, only to the right, or no hedges at all. You will pass by some footpath signs – just continue until you reach the edge of Nun Wood.

3) Turn left here and walk slightly downhill, keeping the wood on your right. On a clear day you can see a long way, down into Buckinghamshire. At the metal gate, circumnavigate the tiny bit of woodland to go around a right hand corner and continue on down with the wood – this time Showsley Wood – on your right. You can see a small lake in the middle of the field, and also a church spire on the horizon far away. Walk past a barn on the left, to a road.

4) Turn left and follow this quiet road into Shutlanger village. When Hayling Cottage is in front of you, go left down the High Street. Just before Baker's Lane

you will see an old chapel on your left. Now turn right down Baker's Lane, passing Butcher's Cottage on the right. Go down the hill, passing a footpath sign on the left, and continue around the corner to the right. At the junction, cross over to Water Lane.

5) Go up here a short distance, noticing a wall which has cleverly been built around a tree root, to avoid damaging it. Turn left at the footpath sign and cross the ridge and furrow field. Go through a kissing gate and continue ahead, until you reach the corner of the field. Cross the footbridge then go up a short incline through a wet, rushy field and through the next gate. Walk up the field, keeping the fence to your right, until you reach the road.

6) Cross the road to a footpath on the other side. Walk up this path, seeing the tower of Stoke Bruerne church quite close up ahead. Follow this path right into the village, up to the church. Go through the metal gate into the churchyard, and as you do so turn to look at the unusual stone on the other side of the right gate post. Pass in front of the church and then to its right, and down a path to a double metal gate. Go through and down to the junction. Turn right here and continue downhill, passing the village green and then the Boat Inn on your left. Just before the hump-backed bridge you can bear left and are now back at the canal, by the locks. Cross over and walk back to the car park.

Coming into Stoke Bruerne Village

PAULERSPURY

This is a pleasant walk through rural south Northamptonshire, although you are surprisingly close to Towcester and the busy A5. There are lots of fine trees to see along the way: from the young specimens in a newly-planted spinney to the magnificent veteran oak trees in Whittlebury Deer Park.

Paulerspury is recorded in the Domesday Book as Paveli's Peri. The grand old house where the Lord lived was Paveli Manor, and the Peri part was probably a reference to the pear orchards in the area. The settlement was almost certainly a staging post along the important Roman road called Watling Street, which is today the busy arterial route the A5.

A famous resident, William Carey, was born in Paulerspury in 1761, and when he grew up he became a shoemaker. He was a keen scholar and taught himself Greek, Latin, Hebrew, French and Dutch. He moved to Moulton, a village close to Northampton, in 1785 and was only allowed to stay after signing a certificate saying he belonged to Paulerspury. This was in case he became a pauper. He later became a famous missionary, translating the Bible into many foreign languages.

During the Industrial Revolution Paulerspury remained almost solely agricultural; the only other significant product being lace (Northamptonshire was once famous for its lace production throughout the county). The community was fairly poor in those times, although today it is a wealthy commuter village for Milton Keynes and London, with a population of around a thousand people.

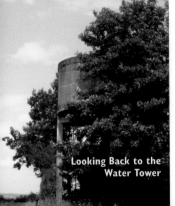

Looking Back to the Water Tower

Another Paulerspury claim to fame is that Queen Elizabeth I and her favourite courtier Sir Walter Raleigh are thought to have stayed in the village on their way back to London.

Whittlebury Deer Park was part of the Royal Forest of Whittlewood, and many of the mighty oaks in the park are hundreds of years old. It is a rare and lovely sight to see so many veteran trees over such a large area, and the holes in the trees are homes to a variety of owls, bats, jackdaws and many other creatures. The park was a royal hunting forest and at that time red deer and fallow deer were brought in especially for hunting, for food and for sport.

Sholebrook Lodge is Grade II listed building, and was formerly the residence of the deputy warden of the Whittlebury Forest. He was clearly very important, to have had such a grand home to live in.

This wintertime photo illustrates the
true magnificence of these mighty oak trees

Detail on Paulerspury
Primary School

Distance in miles and km: 4.5 miles (7 km)

Gradient: Some short inclines but mainly flat level going

Severity: Easy

Approx min time to walk: 1.5 – 2 hours

Stiles: 1 double & 1 single

Maps: OS Landranger 152 or Explorer 207

Path Description: Mainly footpath, bridleway and surfaced tracks

Start Point: Paulerspury church SP 716455 NN12 7NE

Parking: In village close to church

Dog friendly: On leads for preference

Public Toilets: None on route, nearest at Barley Mow pub

Nearest food: Barley Mow pub or Vine House restaurant

THE BASICS

1) Take the footpath to the right of St James the Great church. At the field go through the gate and turn left. Follow the footpath gently downhill, over the footbridge. Here the path divides — take the right-hand path and follow it to a road. You are now in Pury End.

2) Go straight over and head up Scrivener's Lane. At the end turn left, then right, down the bridleway. The fields around here sometimes contain alpacas, so look out for these peculiar, woolly beasts of all shapes and sizes. Go through a gate and onto a grassy track with a hedge either side. You will pass a water tower on your right.

Pury End

3) Go through another gate and keep walking, noticing the young tree belt on your left. This contains a wide variety of trees including oak, ash, beech, pine and larch. Larch is our only deciduous conifer, losing its needles every autumn. It has very distinctive brown cones. Carry straight on up a tarmac track, passing Grange Farm on your left.

4) Passing the corner of Longhedge Wood on your right, ignore the footpath fork on your right. Continue straight on and past a small wood on your left. Go through the gate, and look left to see Sholebrook Lodge among the trees. At the road follow the bridleway straight through the middle of the wood, which is where some lovely tall oak trees grow.

5) At the end of the wood turn left along the road, passing by Sholebrook Lodge again. On your right you can see many wonderful veteran oak trees in Whittlebury Deer Park. At a fork bear left, passing a tall stand of Scots pine trees. Go through the gate, and by the next (permanently open) gate the bridleway leaves the track and winds through the left-hand side of a young spinney of trees. At a field continue ahead, with the hedge to your right. At times you see glimpses of more of the ancient oaks in Whittlebury Park, some of which are truly amazing.

6) At the next field gates go through the gap and straight across the middle of the field in front of you, heading for the far right corner. Buckingham Thick Copse is on your right.

7) At the corner of the field is a huge dead oak tree. Go through the kissing gate and turn left. The footpath skirts around the left of a small field then comes to a gap, with a wood on the right. In front of you is the start of a hedge. Keep to the right of this hedge and follow it all the way down to another gap between fields. Go straight over the next field, heading towards some farm buildings in the distance,

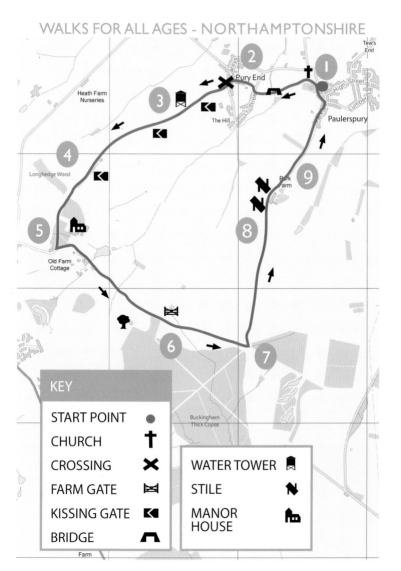

KEY

START POINT	●
CHURCH	†
CROSSING	✕
FARM GATE	⊠
KISSING GATE	◤
BRIDGE	⌒

WATER TOWER	▨
STILE	⦚
MANOR HOUSE	🏠

one with a clock on it. Go through the gap in the hedge and diagonally left across the next small field, heading towards the right-hand corner of a small horse exercise area.

8) Go up the embankment and walk into the farmyard. You are now at Park Farm. Turn left in front of an oil tank, and walk towards a cottage. To the right of the cottage is a wooden gate, which you go through and turn right, heading towards a hedge. Cross the stile and straight over the next field to another stile, a double one. Now turn right and walk the 35 yards (30m) to the road.

9) Turn left and head back towards the village. You will pass Paulerspury House on your left, with huge pine trees in the garden. You also pass The Thatches cottage on your left. At the junction turn left, and walk back to the start.

KING'S CLIFFE

This walk takes you through the absolute heart of Rockingham Forest, a former royal hunting forest. It has easy sections of surfaced trail coupled with slightly more challenging sections of short hills, and there are two stiles.

Footbridge

There is a short flight of eight steps to climb early on in the walk, soon after crossing over Willow Brook. There is an opportunity to do either a shorter (4 miles/6.5 km) or a longer (6 miles/10km) walk.

In Saxon times the village was called Clive, meaning "on the bank of a river". After the Norman Conquest King William made Clive into a Royal Manor. It thus became King's Clive, and then later Cliffe. Clive House, an imposing building along West Street, refers back to the original name of the village.

Hall Yard farmhouse was built in 1603, and it was here that William Law, Kings Cliffe's most distinguished resident, came to live in 1740. He was an important theologian whose work is still read today. He also established charitable foundations in the village, including schools and almshouses.

It will be no surprise that because of its location, wood turning and carving were the main cottage industries in Kings Cliffe for several centuries. Stone was also quarried locally, for building use. In a way, the village has come full circle in becoming part of the Transition Movement, which is a community-led response to the pressures of climate change, fossil fuel depletion and economic decline. It aims to promote and implement more sustainable ways of life, such as using less electricity and helping rural businesses to thrive.

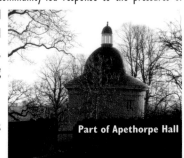
Part of Apethorpe Hall

The small village of Apethorpe was

acquired in the late 15th century by Sir Guy Wolston, and he soon began the construction of the impressive Apethorpe Hall. Queen Elizabeth I, King James I and King Charles I are all known to have visited. In the Second World War it was a sanatorium for wounded soldiers, and after that became a school. After years of neglect and decay it was taken on by English Heritage, who have begun the enormous task of restoring it. It is normally open from Easter to September – look at the English Heritage website for details. It is well worth a visit.

And from the huge to the tiny – Apethorpe's defunct red telephone box now houses a community library, so be sure to take a look at this quirky feature if you go into the village.

Cottage at Apethorpe

Apethorpe's Library

THE BASICS

Distance in miles and km: 4 and 6 miles (6.5 or 10 km)

Gradient: Some short inclines but mainly flat level going.

Severity: Easy but with eight steps up near the start

Approx min time to walk: 2 hours short walk. 3 hours long walk

Stiles: 2

Maps: OS Landranger 141 & Explorer 224

Path description: Mainly footpaths, & bridleways. Some tarmaced tracks

Start Point: Kings Cliffe church TL 007972 PE8 6AX

Parking: In village, on road by church

Dog friendly: On leads for preference

Public Toilets: None on route, nearest at Cross Keys or King's Arms

Nearest food: Cross Keys Inn, King's Cliffe or King's Arms, Apethorpe

1) At the Church, look down the hill to find Hall Yard and follow this down, past the stone "erected by subscription" and past the old water mill. Cross the Willow Brook via the footbridge, then go up the bank with eight steps cut into it, which brings you out onto a track. Turn left here. Very soon take a footpath on your right, and walk up a short incline to a wooden gate. If you look back here you can see King's Cliffe nestling in the valley.

2) Continue ahead, then over a stile and straight over the next field, to a gate. You can see several woods from here, and perhaps make out the shape of an old clay pit to your left. Go down the hill on the hard track and then over a footbridge and up a gentle hill on the other side. After the gate, walk up a wide grass headland to a road. Go over the footbridge and continue straight ahead, with a linear wood close by on the right. You will reach a road.

This way for short route

3) From here it would take you two minutes to walk into Apethorpe village, if you wanted a look round or to visit the Kings Head pub. Otherwise, for the shorter walk turn right here and head up the road, towards Tomlin Wood. Follow this path all the way around to Spa Farm Cottages, and then go to (7).

To do the longer walk go straight over, passing some horse chestnut trees behind the stone wall on your left. You will pass a strange building on your left that is part of the magnificent Apethorpe Hall. You then pass a Scots pine plantation on the left.

At a metal gate you can see a tall poplar plantation in the distance. Continue round the bend and past some tall leylandii trees. When the hedge on the left disappears, you can clearly see New Wood close by. Continue along the road, towards Cheeseman's Lodge. It is very peaceful here, and you are in a very good area for red kites, so do look out and listen for them.

4) Just before the lodge, take the diverted bridleway on your right. Follow the track round and past the lake. Go left over the bridge, then pass between a hedge and walk towards the Lodge Farm buildings. At the big barn turn right and follow the road up, with Tomlin Wood ahead on your right.

5) At the junction bear left then right, along a track with Tomlin Wood immediately on your right.

6) When nearly at the end of the wood

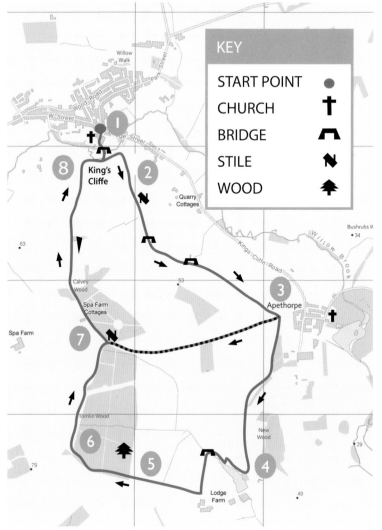

KEY

START POINT	●
CHURCH	✝
BRIDGE	⌐¬
STILE	N
WOOD	🌲

you'll see a sign pointing right. You should take this, noticing the incredible diamond-shaped shapes on the bark of the poplar trees here. Walk up the slight hill, following the path as it hugs the side of the wood. At the road go over a stile (or scramble down a short bank) and turn left. Walk up the tarmac road to Spa Farm Cottages, ignoring the fork to the left.

7) Keeping the cottages to the left, pass under a very tall eucalyptus tree, go over a stile and continue through a small oak wood, going slightly downhill. At a fence corner follow the path to the right, keeping the fence on the left. You can now see King's Cliffe village ahead. Carry straight on and down the hill.

8) At the track turn right, then soon you'll be turning left and going back down the steps you climbed earlier, over the brook and back to the church.

LITCHBOROUGH

This walk takes in the secluded countryside surrounding Litchborough and Farthingstone. Using the footpaths you will come across several inclines, but they are only mildly taxing in the scheme of things. The village lanes you follow are level and the going is easy.

St Martin's church dates mainly from the 13th and 14th centuries, and is Grade II* listed. It is a fine example of the architecture of this period, and is worth a closer look. If you are around on a summer Sunday afternoon then do try the tea and cakes that are served here. The proceeds go towards the upkeep of the church.

St Martin's Church

Litchborough Hall is a Grade II listed building dating from the 17th century. The architecture is amazing. It also has lovely gardens, parkland and woodlands. Occasionally these gardens are open to the public, along with other village gardens (for details look at the National Gardens Scheme Yellow Book or website).

Joy Mead Building

Between the villages you may see buzzards as they circle the skies above, and hear their mewing calls. They favour this undulating landscape, with small copses of trees for nesting in.

In Farthingstone, if you go through the wrought iron gate into Joy Mead Gardens you will enter another world. There is a small temple overlooking a large lawn and flower beds. There are also extensive stone cloisters, which feel cool and spacious. The gardens were created by the Agnew family in 1922 in memory of their two children who died at a young age. The Agnews left the gardens in trust, for all the villagers to enjoy and look after.

The King's Arms pub in Farthingstone has a very unusual, award-winning garden. Many visitors come in spring and summer to look at its quirky features, such as flowers made out of old tyres and tin cans. Herbs and vegetables are grown for use in the pub kitchen. Wildlife

King's Arms

is also catered for, with more than twenty types of butterfly and fifty different species of bird recorded as having visited.

You will walk past Farthingstone village hall, an ornate Victorian building which was the village school from 1877 until its closure in 1962. It was then reincarnated as the village hall, where locals can have a go at anything from "am dram" to yoga.

A little further along is Pansion Row, with broken bottles and china, clinker and oyster shells embedded into the plaster. It would be interesting to hear what inspired this form of decoration!

Distance in miles and km: 3.5 miles (5.5 km)

Gradient: Some short, sharp inclines

Severity: Easy

Approx min time to walk: 1.5 – 2 hours

Stiles: 7

Maps: OS Landranger 152, Explorer 207

Path description: Mainly open countryside, pavements in villages

Start Point: Red Lion pub, Litchborough SP 633544

Parking: On street near pub

Dog friendly: On leads for preference

Public Toilets: Pub in Litchborough

Nearest food: Red Lion, Litchborough or King's Arms, Farthingstone

LITCHBOROUGH WALK

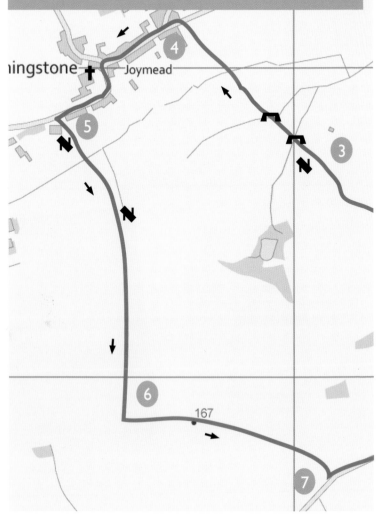

1) Starting with your back to the Red Lion pub turn right and walk down past the war memorial and Ivens Lane. Go past the wrought iron gates of Litchborough House, passing two quite differently-shaped monkey puzzle trees. Turn right down Kiln Lane past a cottage with mullioned windows and on to the Knightley Way. Follow the grassy path between raised beds and two close hedges. Cross the stile and pass in front of the Wellingtonia tree.

2) Head right immediately, down a slight slope to the corner of the field. This is the first of many ridge and furrow fields that you will cross on this walk. Go over the footbridge and stile and walk up a gentle incline in the next field, keeping the hedge close to the right. You go past some magnificent pine trees, to come to a double kissing gate. Next head diagonally left, passing Church Farm buildings, to a gate in the

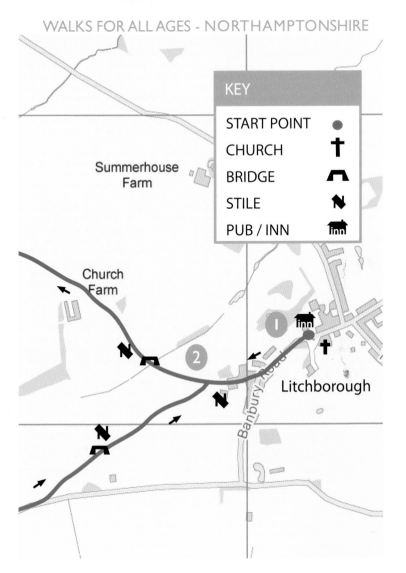

hedge. Farthingstone lies ahead of you, nestling in the gently rolling landscape.

3) Carry on diagonally left to another gate. Bear left across a short section of field to a gap, after which you should bear right and walk down a slight hill to a stile in the hedge. Cross over a tiny footbridge and then go straight across the next field, reaching a footbridge. Bear diagonally left across the next two

fields, in the second one heading for some farm buildings, keeping them to your left. Go through a fenced area to emerge at the road. You are now in Farthingstone.

4) Turn left and walk up the street, passing Manor Farm entrance on the right. Next you will come to Joy Mead Gardens on your left. Do go in and have a look around this unusual place with its well-preserved buildings. After this, you

arrive at the Church of St Mary the Virgin, which is again worth exploring, together with the churchyard. You could also find refreshment at the King's Arms pub, with its not-to-be-missed garden, including some strange "plants"!

Next you should turn left and go down Maidford Road, passing the village hall and quirky Pansion Row with its pieces of coloured pot stuck onto the walls. Continue along past Wheelwright's Cottage, and after Little Court Cottage there is a solid black wooden gate which you need to pass through.

5) Go over the stile and diagonally left over a small paddock to another stile. Then go downhill to a couple of gates. Now walk diagonally uphill to the corner of the field, over a stile and then straight on up a gentle hill in the next field. At a gap in the hedge continue straight on to the next hedge.

6) At this hedge, do not cross over the footbridge but turn left and walk along the headland, keeping the hedge on your right initially, after which it changes to your left. Carry on to the road.

7) At the road turn left and walk along the verge, soon coming to a footpath sign on the left. Go through the gate, turn right and walk around the edge of the field to a footbridge and stile in the hedge. Cross the next field diagonally left, heading towards the village. At a gap in the fence continue ahead, with some horse paddock fencing on your right. Ahead is the tall Wellingtonia tree you passed much earlier. Go back over the stile, down the narrow path and back out on to Kiln Lane. Turn left at the top of the road and walk back past Litchborough House and to the start.

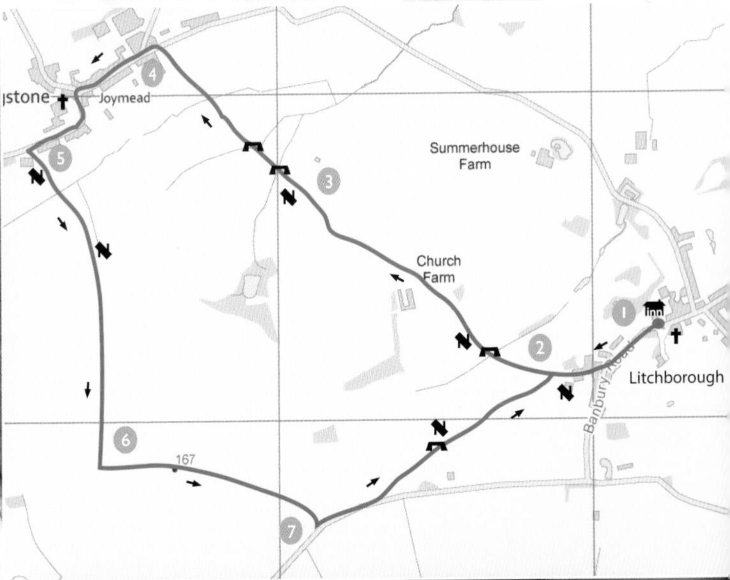
stone
Joymead
Summerhouse Farm
Church Farm
Litchborough
Banbury Road
inn
167
1
2
3
4
5
6
7

WEEDON LOIS

Weedon Lois is a small village on the side of the upper Tove valley, not far from Weston, its sister settlement. "Lois" is said to come from "St Loys", the name of a spring discovered in early medieval times which was thought to have healing properties. A well was created here, and pilgrims came from far and wide to try the waters.

The remains of a much earlier settlement have been found to the south of the village, which is now a site of archaeological interest. The part of the field known as Church Close contains the very well-preserved medieval fish ponds which are said to be from an 11th-century priory, and which you will pass at the end of the walk.

The parish church of St Peter and St Mary's looks out over Church Meadow. This Grade II* listed building dates from about 1100. It was part of the priory linked to the Abbey of St Lucien in Normandy. The priory closed in 1414, but as you can see, the church still remains today.

Medieval Fish pond

There is a very weathered gravestone in the churchyard showing a woman handing a cup to her husband. The story goes that the cup contained poison. The husband died and the woman was later burnt at the stake in a field close to the village. She is supposedly the last person to die at the stake in England.

Weston is proud to possess one of the oldest Baptist chapels in Northamptonshire. It was built in 1791, and before this all baptisms had taken place in an open air baptistery at a farm in nearby Woodend.

Sir Sacheverell Sitwell lived in Weston Hall from 1927 until his death in 1988. He was the younger brother of Dame Edith Sitwell and Osbert Sitwell. A bronze plaque in the churchyard extension — which you will pass on your return to the village — is dedicated to Edith Sitwell. Sculpted by Henry Moore, it depicts the hands of Youth and Age.

Barlye Furlonge Cottage

CATTLEFORD HOUSE

Confusingly, Weedon Lois is mostly called Lois Weedon by the locals, although all modern maps and signposts call it the former, so why this should be is a mystery. Together with Weston a single community is formed, with Weston having the pub and Weedon Lois the church, and the school being happily nestled between the two.

THE BASICS

Distance in miles and km: 3 miles (5 km)

Gradient: Some short inclines but mainly flat level going

Severity: Slightly more difficult but only due to stiles

Approx min time to walk: 1 – 1.5 hours

Stiles: 9

Maps: OS Landranger 152, Explorer 207

Path description: Mainly open countryside, some pavements in villages

Start Point: St Peter and St Mary's church, Weedon Lois SP 602470

Parking: In village, near church

Dog friendly: On leads for preference

Public Toilets: Crown Inn, Weston

Nearest food: Crown Inn, Weston

WEEDON LOIS WALK

1) Facing the old milk churn stand by the church, turn left and walk down to the first road on the right, down Kettle End and past Cattleford House. Go up a grassy hill to the start of the footpath. Cross the stile and footbridge and head straight on up, with a wooded area to the right. The wood soon turns into a hedge. When you come to one big and two small trees in the hedge, look left to see a footpath running out across the field. Take this, and head for the corner of a hedge.

2) Continue along until you reach the road. Cross to the stile opposite and walk diagonally left over a ridge and furrow field. You may find grazing livestock here, such as ponies. At the corner, cross the stile and go straight down between two small spinneys of trees.

3) Go over a stile in the hedge on the right, then turn left and walk the short distance to another stile in the fence. Walk downhill, aiming for the next stile. Now go straight ahead, passing an old oak tree on your right-hand side and follow the path down into Weston village, emerging opposite the Crown Inn.

4) If you want to explore the village then

Pound House, Weston

turn right and have a wander. Otherwise, turn left at the Crown and walk up the street. At the green grass triangle go right, passing in front of Ridgeway Cottage. Keep following the track around to the right, coming to a footpath running alongside a stream.

5) Soon cross a footbridge on the right, then turn left and follow the path with the stream on your left. Now walk through a series of paddocks, going through two gates and over a stile. At the next gap and footbridge go right over a grassed area and then turn left to keep the stream to your left.

Footbridge out of Weston

6) Next cross over a V-shaped structure in the fence and then continue to meander through this rough grassland. Go through a metal gate with a wildlife observation tower close by. Wander through more rough grassland, with willow trees down to your left. Go through a gate to a track, then turn left and walk up the slight hill. Sheep often graze this historic landscape.

7) When you are almost at the gate, turn right at the footpath sign pointing down the hill and walk down, more or less

KEY

START POINT	●
CHURCH	†
BRIDGE	⌐⌐
STILE	⋈
GATE	⋈

following a line of telegraph poles. You are heading for the far corner. This is a great opportunity to admire the view, and to spot Wappenham church on the horizon. When you reach the bottom corner do not go over the footbridge but take the stile in the left-hand hedge, then turn immediately right and go over a footbridge.

8) Turn left after this and head up the edge of the field. Go over a stile and straight on up a gentle hill. You can soon see some reed-beds, indicating the medieval fish ponds on the other side. Follow the fence round to a metal gate and cross the footbridge. Walk straight over the next field, heading for a thatched cottage. Now is your opportunity to look back and see the three fish ponds. Just before the thatched cottage is a stile, after which you walk up between some trees to the road. Turn left and walk back to the start.

GRETTON

This walk is through a peaceful part of the north Northamptonshire countryside, a small strip sandwiched between Corby and the Rutland border to the north.

Almost the entire route is level and easy going, with only four stiles to negotiate. There is some track walking; the rest is on grass or across a mixture of pasture and arable fields.

As you walk you may find it hard to believe you are only 3 miles (5 km) from Corby, as there is a line of low hills which keeps this conurbation out of sight. If you can hear the droning of motorbikes coming from the Rockingham race circuit as you set out, do not despair, as any noise very quickly fades away and you are left with the peace and tranquillity of this undisturbed area.

Gretton was once the third largest village in Rockingham Forest; perhaps an indication of this is that it still benefits from an amazing three public houses, out of a former seven. Most noteworthy historically is the Hatton Arms, which dates back to the early 14th century. It was formerly a gatehouse and is the second oldest pub in Northamptonshire, and the oldest domestic building in Gretton.

Gretton is unusual in having retained its stocks and whipping post, which you will see when you pass the village green. The last recorded use was in 1858 when a villager was put in the stocks for six hours after refusing to pay a fine for drunkenness.

Many buildings with former uses are now private dwellings, such as the Old Schoolhouse, which was built in 1853 by Lord of the Manor Lord Winchilsea. Also look out for Blacksmith's Cottage and Workhouse Cottage. Alternatively, Gretton House in the High Street was a family home until World War II when it was requisitioned by the War Office and became a military hospital. Today it is a home for people with learning difficulties.

Harringworth Lodge

Harringworth Lodge is a Grade II* listed building with 13th-century origins, and was built as a hunting lodge for the deer park created by William do Cantelupe in 1234. The lake adjacent to the lodge was a fish pond which was probably part of the original park.

You will pass several woods with "coppice" in their name. Coppicing was a traditional way of managing woodlands, producing small poles of wood for a variety of uses, such as firewood for charcoal making or heating dwellings, or for making baskets and thatching spars.

THE BASICS

Distance in miles and km: 5 miles (8 km)

Gradient: Almost entirely level, with one short, sharp bank

Severity: Easy

Approx min time to walk: 2 – 2.5 hours

Stiles: 4

Maps: OS Landranger 141, Explorer 224

Path description: Mainly open countryside

Start Point: St James's Church, Gretton SP 898945

Parking: In village near church

Dog friendly: On leads for preference

Public Toilets: None on route, nearest at Lydia's coffee shop

Nearest food: Three pubs in Gretton, or Lydia's coffee shop

1) With your back to St James's Church, turn left and head up the hill, coming to Caistor Road which is opposite. Go up here and at the end turn left, walking past the village hall, with its unusual display of Wellingtons! Pass the pocket park, and at a wooden bridleway sign pointing right, go down the track opposite.

2) When you come to some farm buildings, look for a gap on your left and walk through a small field of newly planted trees, to a gate. You emerge at the top of a short, steep bank, from where you can admire the lovely views, including Morcott windmill on the horizon. Go down the bank and straight over the field to a gate, then across the next field to a gate in the corner.

3) Take the gate immediately on your left, and head straight on across this big

KEY

START POINT	●
CHURCH	✝
BRIDGE	⌐
STILE	⋈
CROSSING	✕
WOODS	♠

field. When the top right-hand corner of the field comes into view you should head for this. When you get there you'll see a stile in the fence to cross, followed by a footbridge. Next, head diagonally left and aim for the rail of a footbridge in the hedge in the distance. This field can be boggy in places, so look out for the rushes, which show you where the wet bits are! Go over the footbridge and stile, and then head diagonally left, to emerge on a track to the left of an area by some piles of soil.

4) Turn right, then go left at the junction (ignoring the Bulwick Estate waymarker discs), to follow a public footpath along the track. After approximately 200 yards (200m) you reach a stile in the fence on the right. Cross over, and head diagonally left across the field. You will pass through into another field, which you should go

straight over, until you reach a stone wall.

5) Turn right and go down the grass track. Cross the wall via the wide stile and follow the path round to the right, passing a lovely dead tree which is growing in what was an old stone pit. Go through a gap and head diagonally right, down to the track by the lake. You will pass an unusual weathervane with a fox on the top, in front of the stately Harringworth Lodge. Go around the head of the lake, and then turn right.

6) Follow the track, from which you get good views of the lake, often with plenty of geese, ducks and swans about. You will pass several blocks of woodland on your left-hand side. The first is Lodge Coppice, followed by Household Coppice.

7) Carry on past the cattle corral on your right, now with Hollow Wood on your left. At another gap between woods the track veers to the right, but you should carry straight on, now walking on grass. The wood on your left is Dryleas Wood, and when this ends, turn right and go through the gap, and then left.

8) At the fence, turn right over the old railway line then through the gate and left, walking with a hedge to your left. Follow the path in front of the woodland and continue in the same field. At the gate turn right, then through the next gate and you are back on the short section you have already walked, which hopefully you recognise!

9) So walk diagonally across the next two fields, coming to the short, steep bank. Go through the gate and head back past the farm buildings, along the track and into the village.

Blue Bell Inn

FREE HOUSE FINE ALES

THE TALBOT

During this north Northamptonshire walk you will explore the tiny village of Wakerley and then cross the county border into Rutland, where you get a tantalising glimpse of Barrowden. Using a combination of footpaths and country lanes, there may be one or two slight inclines, but nothing at all strenuous.

Wakerley lies within the heart of the ancient Forest of Rockingham. If you are wondering where all the trees are, "forest" actually meant an area of land that was used for hunting, rather than referring to an exclusively wooded area.

Former Calcining Kilns

In the Neolithic period, this area was highly important for iron smelting. This is because ironstone, from which iron ore is extracted, is abundant here, and indeed it has been quarried ever since. In the recent past — the 1940s — a quarry firm built a row of four calcining kilns nearby, which you will pass early on in the walk. These strange structures were intended for use in iron extraction, prior to transport to the nearby Corby Steelworks. However, it is believed that the kilns were never actually used, and in fact only two out of the four were ever completed.

Wakerley's Church of St John the Baptist is quite special, originating from the 12th Century, and having the accolade of being Grade 1 listed. After being used for hundreds of years, it was finally declared redundant in 1972 and is now in the care of the Churches Conservation Trust. Among the artefacts inside are floor tablets commemorating the sons of the Earl of Exeter. This Earl was Lord of the Manor of Wakerley, and spent a lot of time here. You will find many references to him in this area, such as Exeter House, which you emerge by after coming down from the church, and the Exeter Arms in Barrowden.

The watermill at Barrowden dates from at least 1259 and it is thought to have been the first form of industry here, around which the settlement developed. Water was harnessed before flowing on into the River Welland, and powered the mill to grind flour, make farm implements and produce leather in the tannery. Sadly, by 1951 the mill was in ruins, and was demolished for safety reasons in 1970.

The Community Shop in Barrowden opened in 2009 after the post office closed. It is run mainly by volunteers, has a tea room and internet access, and is a great asset to the village.

Barrowden Duck pond

The Exeter Arms

THE BASICS

Distance in miles and km: 2.5 miles (4 km)

Gradient: Some short inclines but mainly flat level going

Severity: Easy

Approx min time to walk: 0.75 – 1 hour

Stiles: 2

Maps: OS Landranger 141, Explorer 234

Path description: Mainly unsurfaced paths, some pavements in villages

Start Point: Phone box in Wakerley, SP 954 995

Parking: Main street in Wakerley

Dog friendly: On leads for preference

Public Toilets: None on route, nearest at Barrowden community shop

Nearest food: Exeter Arms, Barrowden, or Barrowden community shop

1) Standing on the pavement facing the phone box, turn right and walk up the main street. You soon pass Wakerley Manor house on your left. Continue ahead, walking past Laurels Farm, on your right. Coming up to the bend you will be able to see two strange towers, the spire of Barrowden Church, and Morcott windmill on the horizon. Follow the road around to the left, and walk up the gentle hill.

Mill Lane

2) Before you reach the right-hand bend you will see a waymarker sign on the left, showing the start of a footpath. Take this, and walk along close to the hedge. You can clearly see the Church of St John the Baptist in the distance. Go through a gap in the hedge into the next field, and carry on, going downhill. Go through the next gap and over the footbridge and continue until you see a stile on the left. You can either follow the footpath left down to the road, or take a very short detour to go and have a look at the historic, Grade I listed church. To do so, continue straight on and go through the gap in the fence and into the churchyard. Retrace your steps after emerging.

3) Go over the stile and down the Jurassic Way to another stile which brings you out onto the road, emerging by Exeter House.

Turn left, and walk down the road on the right. Go over the bridge and you are now officially in Rutland, as you can see from the road and footpath signs! The River Welland marks the boundary between the two counties.

4) Take the footpath on the left and go diagonally right across the field, over the footbridge and continue diagonally right up the hill, straightening out to walk parallel to the Welland, some way above it. Cross a concrete track and continue. After the telegraph pole is a kissing gate in the hedge on the right. Go through this and walk through a grass area to another gate. Follow the path round to the right and through the next gate. Now cross a small field and you will emerge by some houses, on Mill Lane. You will see a finger post pointing left. To continue the walk you should take this, but if you want to explore Barrowden village, now is the time to do so. You could go up to the community shop for some refreshment, or walk a little further to find the pub, which overlooks the village pond.

5) Back at Mill Lane, pass Hay Barn cottage with its triangular windows — former vents in the barn — and walk

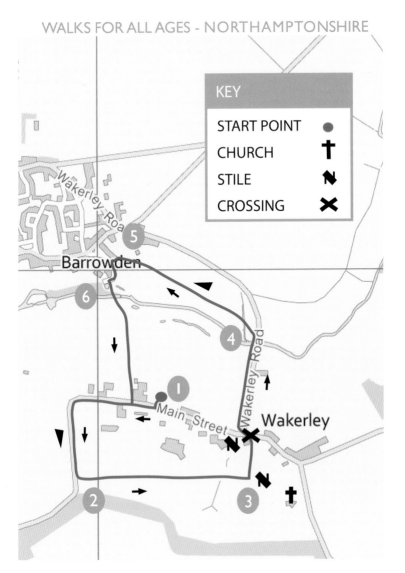

KEY

START POINT ●

CHURCH ✝

STILE ⚑

CROSSING ✕

Wakerley Road

Barrowden

Wakerley Road

Main Street

Wakerley

down between two black metal posts. Soon you walk past the site of Barrowden Mill, where there is a panel you can read which explains the history of the mill and lots of interesting facts about Barrowden. You can also still see the millpond. Take the footbridge over the Welland, and you are once more back on Northamptonshire soil. Once again you can see those mysterious towers . . . You can find out what they are in the text on the previous pages.

6) Go through the gate and straight across the field, avoiding any boggy bits, and heading for the railway arch. This bridge is a remnant from the now disused Peterborough to Corby railway line, which was crucial in the development of Corby's steelworks. Walk up past the farm to the road. Now all you have to do is turn left and walk the short distance back to the start.

EAST HADDON

This varied walk begins by following footpaths crossing pastures and paddocks, then a stretch of surfaced road and track walking, finishing off back on footpaths. There are a few inclines, which are mostly downhill, with a short stretch of uphill on the return route.

You will walk past Holdenby House, so could easily combine this walk with a visit to this impressive place, if you check out the opening times first.

The Church of St Mary is the oldest building in East Haddon, dating from the 12th century. Originally having four bells, a fifth was added later. The first ever recorded peal of five bells anywhere in the country took place here in 1756 – up to this point churches only had four bells. There are now six bells and they make a beautiful noise.

Milk Churns

The head offices and Show Gardens of Haddonstone, a garden ornament company, have been based in East Haddon since 1971. Imposing stone lions sit outside the entrance, presumably on guard! The gardens are open to the public all year round on most weekdays, free of charge. The Jubilee Gardens just over the road from here include a temple and a gothic grotto.

Holdenby Palace was built in 1583 by Sir Christopher Hatton. It was the largest private house in Elizabethan England, having 123 huge glass windows around two courtyards. The house passed down the royal line, and eventually into the ownership of the Lowther family, by which time it was much reduced in size. The Lowther family dates from AD 940 and has produced more Members of Parliament than any other family in England.

Holdenby House is well hidden from the road, and you only get a glimpse of it on this walk. It is worth visiting for its gardens alone, which include a walled kitchen garden with the original Victorian greenhouses. The gardens are open to the public on Sundays and Bank Holiday Mondays from Easter to September. Occasionally the house is also open. There is also a Falconry Centre here.

The National Lift Tower that you can see towards the end of the walk was opened in 1982, and has the local name of the "Northampton Lighthouse". It is 418 feet (127.45m) tall. It was used for testing lifts but closed in 1999, only to be bought by another company, restored, and re-opened for use in 2010. It is the only tower of its kind in this country.

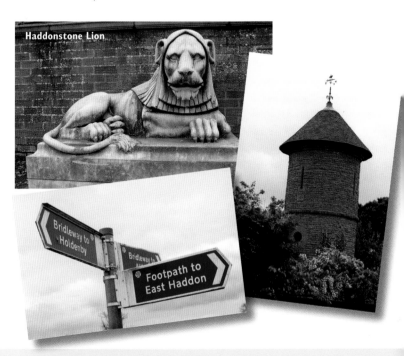

Haddonstone Lion

Bridleway to Holdenby

Bridleway to

Footpath to East Haddon

Distance in miles and km: 5.5 miles (9 km)

Gradient: Some short inclines but mainly flat level going

Severity: More challenging due to distance and stiles, but terrain easy

Approx min time to walk: 2 – 2.5 hours

Stiles: 7

Maps: OS Landranger 152 & Explorer 223

Path description: Footpaths, surfaced and unsurfaced tracks

Start Point: Red Lion Hotel, East Haddon SP 671683

Parking: On street near to hotel

Dog friendly: On leads for preference

Public Toilets: None on route, nearest at Red Lion Hotel

Nearest food: Red Lion Hotel

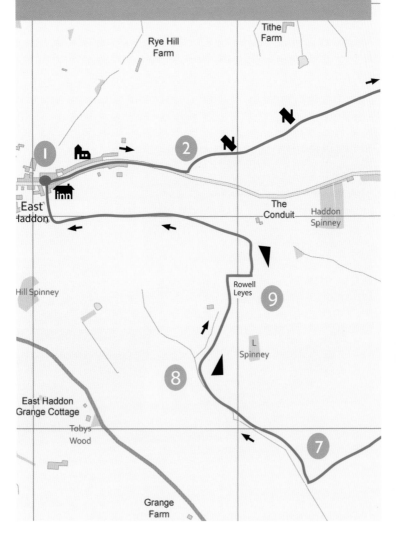

1) With your back to the Red Lion Hotel, turn left and walk along the pavement. You will pass the Old Chapel, now a private house. Ignore a footpath sign on the left and continue walking along the road.

2) Turn left up a track and immediately take the footpath on the right. Go straight across the field, aiming for any gap in the very straggly hedge and walk on to cross over a stile. Now bear slightly left,

heading for the oak tree furthest to the right in a line of trees ahead. Keep on to reach the stile, and once over, walk with a hedge to the right, admiring the extensive views.

3) Ignore a bridleway coming in from the right, and continue to walk close to the hedge, heading for the farm buildings of Holdenby North Lodge. Cross over into the paddock and head straight

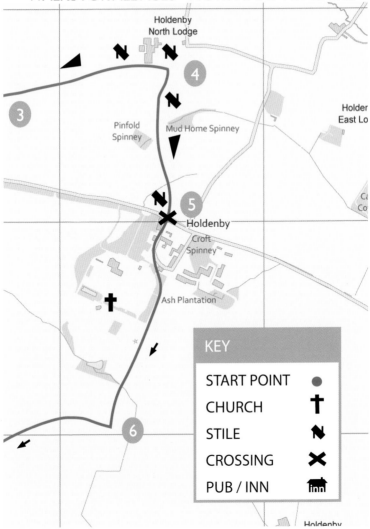

Holdenby
North Lodge

4

3

Holder
East Lo

Pinfold
Spinney

Mud Home Spinney

5

Holdenby

Croft
Spinney

Ca
Co

Ash Plantation

6

Holdenby

KEY

START POINT	●
CHURCH	✝
STILE	⚑
CROSSING	✖
PUB / INN	🏠

across to a metal gate into the farmyard. Turn right and walk past a barn to the corner of two fences. Cross the stile and keeping the fence to your right, you quickly come to another stile on the right. You are now on the Macmillan Way.

4) Go down a slight slope and up the other side to a stile. Now head left down this ridge and furrow field to a stile in the fence. This landscape has a real parkland feel to it, and no wonder, because you are walking in the Holdenby Estate. Head up the slight incline and straight across, aiming for a metal gate below. In the next field aim for another metal gate straight ahead. Cross the stile, to emerge in front of Holdenby Lodge House.

5) Go up the road opposite, past Home Farm House and the Schools Centre. Follow the road round to the left, and at the

historic church sign turn right. Go through the gate and head straight down the track, ignoring the bridleway sign on the left. Now is your chance to visit the historic All Saints Church, should you wish to do so. Otherwise, go through the gate and continue down the track to a gate by a thin strip of woodland, and straight on.

6) Follow the track as it bends to the right, walking around the edge of this very large field, and then walk straight across the next field.

7) At the junction of footpaths go right to East Haddon. Continue through the gap in the hedge, bearing left. The line of oak trees in the field to the right is probably all that's left of an old hedge line. At the next field continue straight ahead, now with the hedge to your right.

8) At a gateway turn right and walk up the hill, past Rowell Leyes, a deserted farmhouse. Follow the bend round and at the top turn right and walk with a hedge to your right.

9) Just before the next field turn left so you are walking downhill with a hedge on the right, towards a farmstead. At the corner turn left and walk next to a line of telegraph poles with the hedge on your right. Go through the gap and continue walking along the field edge. If you look to the left you can now truly see for miles — see if you can spot the National Lift Tower in Northampton. Continue walking straight on, until you reach the recreation ground. Head for the pavilion, leaving the field by way of a gap just before you get to it. Turn right down the track, to emerge at the pub.

The view from the stile, looking towards Holdenby

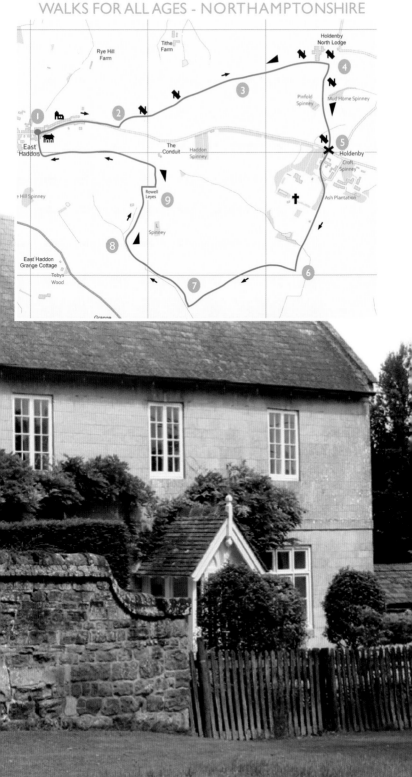

In this walk you visit the sister villages of Little and Great Brington, and the neighbouring hamlet of Nobottle. You will walk on tracks, bridleways and footpaths, with a small amount of lane walking in the villages.

There are only gentle inclines, and you will see some great views. If you do this walk in July or August you could visit nearby Althorp House afterwards, perhaps treating yourself to afternoon tea.

Althorp House is the family home of nineteen generations of the Spencer family, one of the most notable members being, of course, Lady Diana Spencer, the late Princess Diana. Built in 1508, the house sits in 550 acres of parkland — complete with large

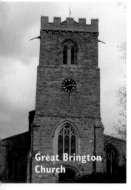

herds of deer. The house, which has stunning décor, is open to the public each summer, and a literary festival is held here most years.

St Mary's church, Great Brington, dates from at least 1220, and it is thought that a wooden church stood on this site prior to burning down in the 13th century. Nineteen generations of the Spencer family are buried here, and because of this some conspiracy theorists believe Diana is also buried here, rather than at Althorp itself.

Great Brington Church

The death of Diana had quite an effect on the village. The pub changed its name from the Fox and Hounds to the Althorp Coaching Inn, and tourists flocked to the area. The Inn dates back to the 16th century, and would have provided sustenance to the many tradesmen who served Althorp House.

Little Brington Church is a strange building to look at, because it has a spire but no nave, or main body of the church. Frederick Spencer built the church as a memorial

to his first wife. Services were held here regularly, but by the 1940s the church had fallen into disrepair. The main body of the church was demolished in 1947, but at the request of the Air Ministry the distinctive tower with its octagonal spire was spared. It had become a landmark to navigators, and likely serves the same purpose today.

The Saracen's Head in Little Brington was built in the 17th century from local Northamptonshire ironstone. The bar has original beams and wooden floors and you could enjoy a meal here, or partake of the real ales on sale.

Nobottle borders the Althorp estate, which owns much of the property in it. There are only thirteen houses, making it one of the smallest hamlets in England.

Dairy Farm, Great Brington

THE BASICS

Distance in miles and km: 4.5 miles (7 km)

Gradient: Some short inclines but mainly flat level going

Severity: Easy

Approx min time to walk: 2 – 2.5 hours

Stiles: 2

Maps: OS Landranger 152 & Explorer 223

Path description: Byway, bridleway, footpath and pavements

Start Point: Saracen's Head, Little Brington SP 663637

Parking: On street near to pub

Dog friendly: On leads for preference

Public Toilets: Nearest at Saracen's Head or Althorp Coaching Inn

Nearest food: Saracen's Head, Lt Brington; Althorp Coaching Inn, Gt Brington

1) With your back to the Saracen's Head turn right and walk up the street. At Old Forge on the corner of Blacksmith's Lane turn left and walk up a slight hill, passing Stoneacre, until you reach the end. Turn left and you soon see a byway sign on the right.

2) Go down here, enjoying the lovely views across south Northamptonshire. Go through a large gap in the hedge and continue ahead, then through another gap and carry on.

Chinkwell Cottage

3) Go through a gate on the left, then head diagonally right across the ridge and furrow field, aiming for the second metal gate to the right. Go through this and head diagonally left across another ridge and furrow field, with New Covert Wood directly to your right, aiming for a metal gate in the top left corner. Go straight across the next small field, over a track and through a gate. You can see West Lodge on the hill to the right. Go through the gap and walk ahead to the next gateway. Grange Farm is up there on the hill to the left. Continue ahead until you reach Nobottle pumping station.

4) Walk up the track to the Main Street, passing Chinkwell Cottage and Townsend Farm. At the junction road turn right, and look for a footpath sign in the left-hand hedge a little further up. Cross the road to this, go over the stile and walk diagonally left to the gateway, where you will pass the westernmost corner of Nobottle Wood. There is a rookery here, and you may well hear the cawing of these large black birds, and see their untidy nests. Now walk up the hill, bearing right to a stile in the hedge. Cross the footbridge and at the road turn right and head on round the bend, ignoring the first footpath sign and taking the next one, which says "Footpath to Great Brington".

5) Go through the gate and head straight across the field, slightly downhill. You will have firstly Harlestone Thicket and then later Harlestone Forest to your right. Continue straight over the next field. Cross over the carriage drive leading to Althorp Park.

6) Continue across the next field to a kissing gate. If you look to the right as you walk across this field you will be able to see all of the imposing Althorp House. Go through the next gate and walk ahead, noticing the houses on your left as you approach the village, which are the old almshouses. Go through a gate and up a lane, to emerge by the Fox and Hounds in Great Brington.

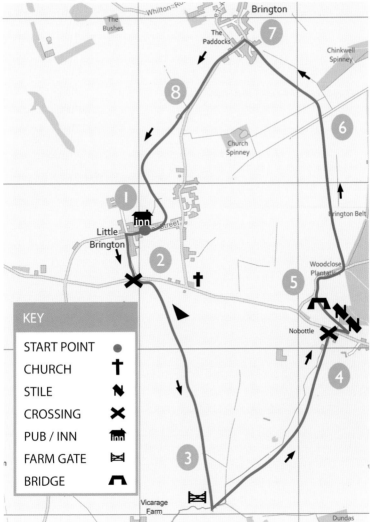

7) If want to visit the impressive St Mary's Church then turn right here. The Old Rectory next door is also worth a look, with its hexagonal tower and many chimneys. It is a huge place — rectors must have been blessed with many children! Otherwise turn left and walk along the pavement out of the village. Cross over the road at the second footpath sign on the right.

8) Keeping close to the left-hand hedge skirt round a large pond, and then bear right to a kissing gate in the hedge. Cross the footbridge and bear right across the next field. After this, go straight across the next field, aiming for the church spire ahead. Little Brington is laid out before you, in all its glory. Follow this path all the way until you reach the road. You have now a very short walk back to the Saracen's Head.

BRAUNSTON

This walk takes you through the very westernmost reaches of Northamptonshire, and in fact you cross the border into Warwickshire during the first half of the walk.

You follow level towpaths, and gently undulating bridleways and footpaths. Your reward will be a very colourful time on the canal sections, with all the brightly painted narrowboats to see, and some amazing views of the countryside.

The whole of this area is rich in industrial archaeology, including the remains of the original route of the Oxford Canal, and two abandoned railway lines. There are also the lost villages of Braunstonbury and Wolfhampcote, which you walk past early on.

Little is known about Braunstonbury, which was regarded as part of Braunston itself as it was never separately listed in taxation records. Wolfhampcote was abandoned in the late 14th century, probably being more or less wiped out by the Black Death brought in by refugees from London, after which any survivors moved away. The most noteworthy surviving structure — amazingly — is the Church of St Peter, which stands all alone, apparently in the middle of nowhere.

St Peter's Church

Braunston itself was originally no great shakes — just a stop-off point on the Oxford Canal. Its fortunes changed in the 1830s when improvements made to the canal network meant it became a key stopping place in the link between the Grand Junction and Oxford canals. Braunston expanded almost overnight, with dozens of businesses such as chandlers, rope-makers, blacksmiths and carpenters setting up in the village. This led to a big demand for food, drink and accommodation, and at one time Braunston had as many as twelve public houses. You can still see the old bakery — just look out for the Hovis sign near the start of the walk.

The Boat Shop

Weedon Line Bridge

The Admiral Nelson pub, on the canal at the end of the village, was built in 1730. It is said to be haunted by a figure in black who walks through walls at the most inconvenient moments. Something to bear in mind should you decide to go for a drink there!

The Stop House was where tolls were collected from boats travelling between the two canals, according to the load they carried. The design of the building enabled the toll man to see boats approaching from either direction. Nowadays it is where the Canal and River Trust (formerly British Waterways) has its office. What a lovely place to work!

The Admiral Nelson

THE BASICS

Distance in miles and km: 6 miles (10 km)

Gradient: Some short inclines but mainly flat level going

Severity: Easy (13 steps up and down at metal footbridge)

Approx min time to walk: 2.5 – 3 hours

Stiles: None

Maps: OS Landranger 152 & Explorer 222

Path description: Towpaths, footpaths, pavements & unmade trackS

Start Point: Old Plough Inn, Braunston SP 540662

Parking: In village close to the Old Plough

Dog friendly: On leads for preference

Public Toilets: None on route

Nearest food: Any of Braunston pubs, or Cake Slice tearoom

1) Walk down Nibbits Lane, almost opposite the Old Plough. You can't help noticing the pleasing mural on an oil tank on the left. The lane soon turns into a path, which takes you straight down to the canal. Cross the humpback bridge and turn right and walk along the towpath, admiring the boats that are moored up. Go over another bridge, and past the Stop House, continuing along until you go under the A45.

2) You should now bear immediately left by a fenced area, then right, down a tarmaced drive, to a cattle grid. Go through the gate ahead of you and follow the track over the stream and round to the right. Keep going. When you reach the church, you have crossed over the border into Warwickshire.

3) Immediately after the church go left down a bridleway, through a gate and under the bridge. The line used to run from Weedon to Leamington Spa. Head across the big field, keeping fairly close to the hedge on the left. When you come to a hedge, carry straight on across the next field, heading for the gap on the horizon. Cross the track and go straight on across the next two fields, until you reach a footbridge.

4) Cross the bridge and bear very slightly right across the next field. You should now be walking quite close to the River Leam — although it appears more like a stream to you and me! Keep following the bridleway ahead. At the very end turn left.

5) Walk down to the footbridge, called the Miry Bridge, which takes you over the River Leam. Then, ignoring the footpath to the right, carry on up a gentle hill. Keep going straight on, hugging the field boundary hedge. Disregard another footpath crossing yours, and soon go through a wide gateway and follow the track downhill. When you come to a track, turn left and go up the hill.

6) Next, walk to the junction then carry straight on; do not go left to Berry Fields. Then, where the track bends around to the right, strike out across the field in front of you, bearing diagonally left, aiming for a point just before the corner of the field. As you walk across this field you can possibly see the furthest you can see on any of these walks.

7) Go through the gap in the hedge and walk downhill through rough grassland, then up through a tiny stretch of woodland. Upon reaching a field, walk uphill with the wood on your left. At the corner of the wood continue straight on to some large trees on the horizon. Go through a gap and follow the path to the A45.

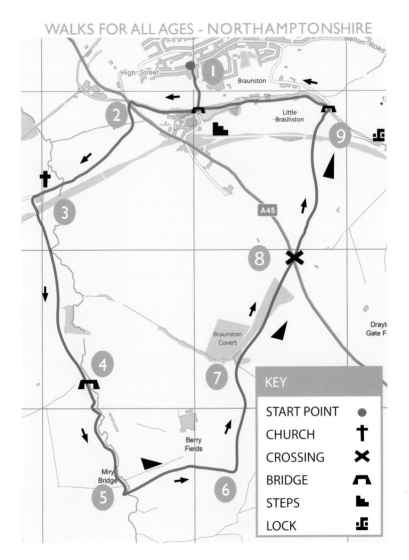

8) Cross over carefully and walk down the track, towards some farm buildings. Ignore a footpath to the left. Keep going all the way downhill, through a gateway and over the old railway bridge. Continue downhill, to emerge at the canal opposite the Admiral Nelson pub.

9) Turn right and then dip left and go under the bridge, heading back towards Braunston. Go past the Crooked Cottage by the lock, and under bridge no. 3. Pass the Boat Shop (or go in and browse through their collection of books and prints). Then carry on walking along the towpath, going under bridge no. 2. Climb the steps of the footbridge which passes over the entrance to the marina. The height gives you a chance to survey all the boats from above. Then, finally, on to bridge no. I, where you leave the towpath, cross the canal and head on back up Nibbits Lane.

WELFORD

You will walk a combination of footpaths, surfaced and unsurfaced tracks and towpaths. You will pass some interesting archaeological sites and see extensive views across Warwickshire and Leicestershire.

Once known as Wellesford, which means "ford by a spring or stream", Welford was an established settlement well before its Domesday Book listing of 1086. Roman pottery has been found in the fields surrounding the village, and mounds and hollows in the fields to the west of the village, through which you walk, are the site of the original settlement. It is thought that Welford originally consisted of three parallel streets. The present West Street with its church and Manor House was probably the main street.

Welford Church Clock

Tumbledown Barn

The Church of St Mary the Virgin dates from the 13th century, was linked to the nearby Sulby Abbey. There are many old graves in the churchyard, and also a granite and bronze memorial (called a Calvary) to the men of Welford and Sulby who died in the First World War. There are some lovely lime trees here, too.

A stone manor house stands directly north of the church, but it is hard to see and appreciate this elegant, two-storeyed building, as it is mostly hidden from view by tall walls. What you can see, above the entrance gate, is a striking sundial with a cordoned pear tree beneath, which is best appreciated at blossom or fruiting time.

In West End, not far from the church, is the Congregational Chapel. This large, square, red-brick building was built in 1793, having been designed to accommodate about 500 people. It did so well that by 1867 a Sunday School building was added to the side of it. Today it is a listed building.

On The Grand Union Canal

Welford is almost exactly halfway between Northampton and Leicester, and used to be an important resting place for stagecoaches travelling between the two, or to London beyond. It had a total of seven inns or coaching houses along the present High Street, along with chandlers, drapers, wheelwrights, bakers, tailors — you name it. It was also served by a short arm of the Grand Union Canal, and has two marinas. While most of these businesses have gone now, the village community is thriving, with dozens of societies and clubs meeting here, often in the large Village Hall or the new Youth and Community Centre. So people should never be bored in Welford!

Village hall

THE BASICS

Distance in miles and km: 4 miles (6.5 km)

Gradient: Some short inclines but mainly flat level going

Severity: Easy

Approx min time to walk: 1.5 — 2 hours

Stiles: 1

Maps: OS Landranger 140 & Explorer 223

Path description: Mainly footpaths, pavements, unmade track & towpaths

Start Point: St Mary the Virgin Church, West St SP 642803

Parking: In village close to church

Dog friendly: On leads for preference

Public Toilets: None on route, nearest at Wharf Inn, Welford

Nearest food: Wharf Inn, Welford

1) With your back to the church turn right and walk down the road, past a sundial on the side of a building, with a pear tree underneath. Carry on past the school, the village hall and Engine House, all the way to the end of West Street.

2) Here take the footpath called the "Welford Walk", which goes left down a track. Go through a gate into a field and bear slightly right across the field. Go through a gateway and straight over the next field. Ignore a footpath to the

right, carrying straight on to a kissing gate, then straight on again. There is a pond to your right, a fish pond from medieval times. Keep close to the houses on your left, and then when you reach the fence corner and a big old tree, look ahead and slightly right, to see a gate, which you should make for. As you walk across the field, notice all the lumps and bumps, showing the site of the old village.

3) Once through the gate, turn right

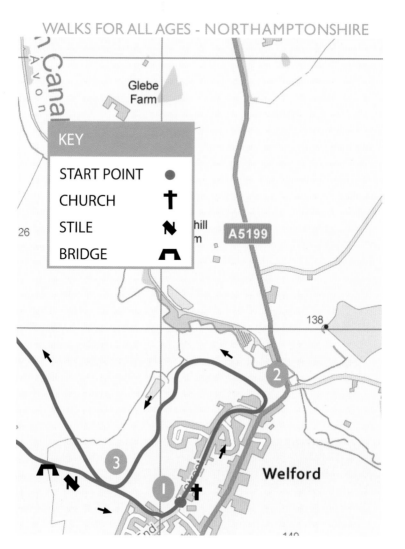

into Hall Lane, which is a bridleway. Walk down this concrete track. This is easy walking and there is no need to worry about navigation just for now.

4) The track finally bends to the right, towards Lodge Farm, but instead you should go straight ahead, now on an unsurfaced path, past a small woodland on your left. At the end of the wood, ignore a track coming in from the left and carry on, with a hedge to your left. There are great views —

across Northamptonshire to your left, Warwickshire ahead and Leicestershire to your right.

Continue through a couple more fields until you read a grass track coming in from the left. Do not take this but do a quick right and left to follow the bridleway straight on, now with a straggly hedge directly to your right. You can see two church spires ahead. The one on the left is South Kilworth and the one on the right is North Kilworth church.

You can also see Stanford reservoir and nature reserve to your left. Walk down until you reach the canal.

5) Cross the bridge, then turn right and pass under the bridge, to reach the towpath. Walk along, passing under bridge 39, and then under bridge 38 come up and turn left over the bridge.

6) Take the footpath immediately on your left on the other side. Follow the path alongside the canal for a short time, then it breaks away to head off up the hill. Go over a footbridge spanning a ditch and continue straight on, with a hedge to the left. Go over a footbridge into the next field and continue up the headland, slightly uphill. At the top ignore a gap to the left but follow the path around to the right, to a metal gate.

7) At the tumbledown red-brick barn turn right and strike out across the field, heading for the top right-hand corner, by a row of trees. Cross over the stream and the stile, then bear diagonally right up the hill, heading for the corner. Again you'll see lots of ancient lumps and bumps — this is the sister field to the one you crossed earlier. Sure enough, at the corner go through the gate and you are back on Hall Lane once more. Turn right and head up the hill, passing Holly Cottage, to come out on West End, opposite the Youth and Community Centre. Walk back to the church.

Turn Left on Bridge 38

ARTHINGWORTH

"Big skies" is the theme of this walk. As soon as you leave the village and start striding across the fields, you will be struck by the vastness of the skies that you can see all around you.

Tollemache Arms

Not that this walk is in any way bleak, as the space is contained by the rolling hills all around. You will walk on a combination of bridleways and footpaths, with some unsurfaced tracks and quiet lanes.

Arthingworth is a small village with many ancient buildings. Church Farm and the well-kept tithe barn can be found just up the road from the church. Arthingworth Manor dates from the mid-18th century and is Grade II listed. It was built for the Rokeby family, and was originally in the shape of an E. It is now a ruin, although its demise led to the discovery of a much older building within.

On your way to Harrington you will encounter the church first, quite far from the village itself as the Great Plague took its toll here and many dwellings were abandoned and subsequently disappeared. It is well worth a look inside the church in order to see the "tuba stentoro-phonica" – or speaking trumpet to you and me – which is one of only eight to be found in the whole country. It is thought these horns were originally invented for speaking between ships at sea. Here, it would have been used for calling people to church.

The Manor of Harrington has had a chequered history, passing through many noble families. Mostly recently it passed into the hands of the Tollemache family, although it was pulled down by Lionel Tollemache in 1745, because he had other estates to maintain and could no longer afford the upkeep.

What does remain is an amazing set of lumps and bumps (which archaeologists call "earthworks") in a field which you walk through. This site is locally called "The Falls" with the "Park" adjoining. You get a fantastic view of all this as you walk downhill towards this archaeologically important site.

Old Barn Near The Falls

Back in the present day, a tiny and independent distillery is housed in a converted barn at Falls Farm. The Warner Edwards distillery makes gin, a key ingredient of which is the spring water, which is gathered from the Falls area. It would be nice to think that the people who lived and worked in the Manor all those years ago would have approved!

Footpath to Harrington

BRAYBROOKE ROAD

Distance in miles and km: 5 miles (8 km)

Gradient: Some short inclines but mainly flat level going

Severity: Easy

Approx min time to walk: 2 – 2.5 hours

Stiles: I single and I double stile

Maps: OS Landranger 141 & Explorer 223

Path description: Mainly footpaths, country lanes and unmade track

Start Point: The Church of St Andrew, Arthingworth SP 755814

Parking: In the village, near the church

Dog friendly: On leads for preference

Public Toilets: Bull's Head, Arthingworth or Tollemache Arms, Harrington

Nearest food: Bull's Head, Arthingworth, or Tollemache Arms, Harrington

THE BASICS

ARTHINGWORTH WALK

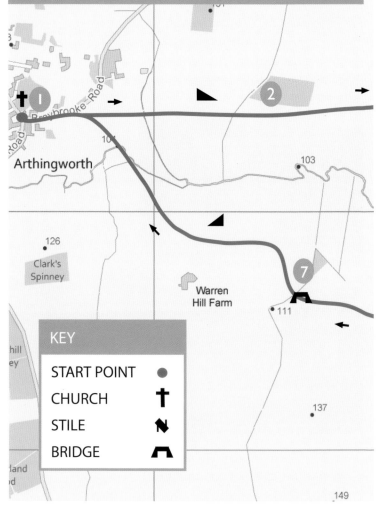

KEY

START POINT	●
CHURCH	✝
STILE	N
BRIDGE	⌒

1) With your back to the church, go left down Braybrooke Road, heading away from the village. At a bridleway post on the right, take the one pointing left. Head diagonally downhill to a gate in the fence. Keep walking until you cross over a concrete bridge. Now bear slightly right over the next field, which is cropped, and up a slight hill. At the next field you go straight on up the hill, bearing slightly left, becoming progressively closer to a line of telegraph poles on the left, and a young

spinney of trees running alongside the field. When you reach the top left-hand corner, go through the gap between two posts.

2) Now walk along the grass of the right-hand edge of a field. This turns into a track. Carry on all the way, admiring the views and the big skies, until you reach a pylon.

3) Here you should bear right on a

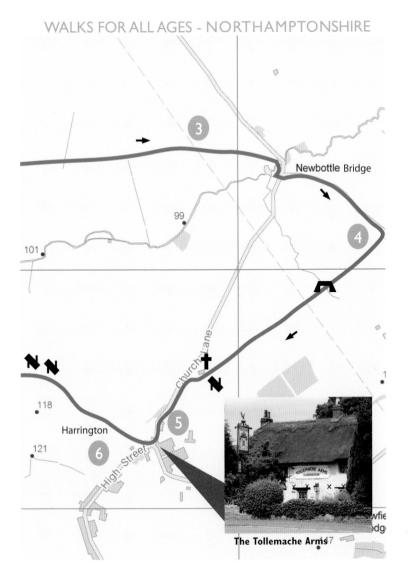

The Tollemache Arms

small path, away from the track. At the end is a footbridge to cross, and then you should turn right, and go over Newbottle Bridge — rebuilt in 1876 — which crosses the River Ise. Immediately go left, towards Thorpe Underwood. Walk up the slight hill, with many mature and twisted oak trees in the hedge to the right.

4) At the top is a footpath sign pointing right, to some brown gates. Before going

through, you could walk a little further up into Thorpe Underwood, to see the rookery in the trees at Cromwell House (Cromwell spent some time in this area). Otherwise, take the small hand gate on the right — the catch is at the top on the other side. Go through a kissing gate and cross the horse paddock to a large wooden gate. Make your way downhill to a wooden footbridge. Harrington church is directly ahead of you. Go up the next field, with the hedge to your left. When you

93

reach a corner of a fenced area, by a line of pine trees, bear right across the field, to a stile in front of the church.

5) Follow the footpath around to the left of the church, and then walk down a lime and beech tree avenue to the road. Turn left. The footpath runs alongside the road, with a hedge in between. You soon come into Harrington village. At the road junction turn right, passing in front of the Tollemache Arms.

6) Take the first footpath on the right, just after the pub. Go through the gate and bear slightly left downhill, aiming for a metal field gate. The lumps and bumps in the field to the left are "The Falls" — the remains of the old Manor House and gardens. Go through the next gate and keep bearing left. The path skirts around the top end of the earthworks to a gap in the hedge. Here you cross a double stile. Go straight across the next field, through a gap in the hedge and straight on again, eventually coming to a footbridge in the far corner of the field.

7) Walk across the next narrow field, go through the gap in the hedge and turn left. Walk up a slight incline. Go through the gate and straight on, with a hedge close to your left. At the next gate bear right and walk down the hill, to the bottom left-hand corner of this grass field. Keep going, crossing over the small red-brick bridge. Then head uphill bearing left, to the corner. At the road turn left and walk back to the church.

This winter photograph clearly shows the scale of the Rookery

ABOUT THE AUTHOR

Walking has been one of my passions since a young age. I'm not sure where it came from, as my family weren't particularly keen on walking (picnics, yes, but not actually walking in the countryside). So from as young an age as 12 I would get my backpack and boots out, cobble together some cheese and tomato sandwiches that always fell apart before I got to the bottom of our road, grab a bottle of water and go (it was my great regret that there was never any ginger beer in our house).

It's hard to say briefly what I love about it, but I'll try. Fresh air. Lovely scenery. Getting away from it all. Healthy, enjoyable, outdoor exercise (and free, at that). A sense of perspective. The camaraderie of walking with family or friends. Getting un-knotted (as opposed to the alternative).

I've moved around a lot, and every county I've lived in has had much to offer for the walker. I genuinely believe the British countryside is among the loveliest on the planet. What better way to experience it, than striding out along its footpaths and byways?
If you have yet to catch the Walking Bug, then I really hope that this book will well and truly infect (or convince) you. It really is all out there for the taking. Best foot forward . . .

Cheryl Joyce.